A DIFFERENT SHADE OF GREEN

A DIFFERENT SHADE OF GREEN

THE ALAN McLOUGHLIN STORY

WITH BRYCE EVANS

Ballpoint Press

To Deby, Abby, Megan,
Mum, Dad & Diane
All My Love Always,
xxxx

And to Bryce.
Thank you for your time, patience
and understanding in
putting my story together.

Published in 2014 by Ballpoint Press
4 Wyndham Park, Bray, Co Wicklow, Republic of Ireland.
Telephone: 00353 86 821 7631
Email: ballpointpress1@gmail.com
Web: www.ballpointpress.ie

ISBN 978-0-992673253

Book design and production by Elly Design

Photographs by Sportsfile; 'The News', Portsmouth;
Dave Evans, Swindon Advertiser;
and Alan McLoughlin's personal collection.

Cover photograph:
Alan McLoughlin celebrates his famous goal against Northern Ireland in Windsor Park, Belfast in November 1993 which secured the Republic of Ireland's qualification for the 1994 World Cup in the USA.
PHOTOGRAPH BY GETTY IMAGES

Printed and bound by GraphyCems

CONTENTS

ABOUT ALAN McLOUGHLIN

Former Republic of Ireland international Alan McLoughlin was born in Manchester of Irish parents. He joined Manchester United as an apprentice but never played for the first team. Following his release from Old Trafford, he finally came of age playing with Swindon, his performances gaining him a late call-up to the Irish squad instead of Gary Waddock in controversial circumstances in 1990.

McLoughlin later played for a number of clubs including Southampton and Wigan but spent the longest part of his career with Portsmouth where he is now first team coach.

He lives in Swindon with his wife Deby
and two daughters Abby and Megan.

1
Red Spots

One Sunday morning in September, 2012...

6:30 in the morning and, with my alarm bleeping, I got out of bed. Slowly. Jesus, I felt tired. As I brushed my teeth I thought back to the previous night. I was so shattered I didn't even make it through Match of the Day, falling asleep on the settee. Now, bleary eyed, I readied myself for another full day of coaching with Portsmouth football club's academy. Sunday should have brought rest, but thanks to staff shortages at the beleaguered club I was due to manage the Under-14s that day.

So tired! The night before, after being woken up by that tinny old Match of the Day end tune, I'd gone to the toilet. I was so wrecked I couldn't even stand up to pee. And I was completely sober. I'd just sat on the toilet, head down, trying to stay awake. Because my head was bowed I was looking into the toilet bowl. Did I see something in my urine? A little bit of red? A red spot? Probably nothing. Your mind plays tricks on you when you're that tired... doesn't it?

That Sunday Pompey's young charges were playing AFC Wimbledon Under-14s. It was a lovely sunny day and, as I drove the minibus up the A3 towards New Malden, I looked into the rear view mirror and smiled. All the parents and kids behind me were in a good mood. There were a few younger lads from the Under-12s and Under-13s that I'd thrown into the team and they seemed to be settling in well. Come 2pm that afternoon, we were back on the minibus and celebrating a win. Wimbledon were bigger, stronger lads, but we passed them off the pitch. The kids played brilliantly. Even the younger boys did everything

I asked of them. And me? I was looking forward to having Monday off and, above all, catching up on a bit of sleep.

We got back to Fratton Park at 4pm. After the long drive I was dying for a wee. The old stadium is eerie when it's dark and empty and so, as I made for the toilets in the away changing room, I was glad that the Portsmouth academy physiotherapist, Lucas McArdle, was also around.

I stood at the urinal and started to pee. This time I didn't need to look down to detect a red speck. There was red everywhere. A hell of a lot of blood.

Shocked, I instinctively jumped back. But the torrent kept coming out of me, deep scarlet in colour. By now I was pissing dark red blood everywhere, my urinary arc cascading all over the place.

'Lucas!' I barked.

He came into the toilets and I watched his expression drop as he caught sight of the bloody pool on the floor.

- 'Lucas, what the fuck is that?'

- 'Macca, go straight to hospital'

• • •

I stayed with Lucas to mop up the mess, the two of us wringing the blood out of the mops in the dark. Cleaning away the blood, beneath the creaking old South Stand, there was an unsettling silence between us. Lucas sensed that I was embarrassed. 'Just make sure you go straight to hospital' was his parting shot.

I left Fratton Park in a daze, got in the car, and phoned my wife Deby. I told her about the blood. We agreed to meet at the hospital in Swindon. It would mean being nearer home and I knew that was where I needed to be. That hour and a half drive back to Swindon from Portsmouth was silent. I always have the radio on in the car; usually, the football jabber on Talksport radio accompanies me on wearying drives. But this time I left it off. I was still in shock and needed to think about what had just happened to me. The silence only accentuated a dull ache in the pit of my stomach, which was becoming increasingly acute.

But it wasn't just the physical pain. There was something else, too; a niggling feeling, an infrequent visitor which I hardly recognised at first: fear.

In the silence and the darkness, my hands clutching the steering wheel as if it was some sort of anchor to normality, I tried to pull myself together. The first tactic which came to mind was to try and remember when the last time was that I had experienced fear like this, and how I had dealt with it then.

And with that, my mind wandered all the way back to November 1993.

One night in November, 1993...

I was sitting on the Republic of Ireland team coach as it wound its way through Belfast when the fear hit me. Similarly, it was completely silent and it was dark, about 7pm in the evening. The bus snaked past mean, red-bricked streets. Dank, claustrophobic housing. Tribal colours fluttering menacingly, illuminated by streetlight. Hostility. Under Jack Charlton's management, the Irish team coach was not usually quiet; there'd be some come-all-ye folk ballad blaring and plenty of craic between the players. But on this occasion, uniquely, the reason for having the lights and sound off was security.

We were travelling to play Northern Ireland in our final qualifying match in the World Cup campaign, a make-or-break game which would decide whether or not we would be travelling to America the following summer to compete in the World Cup finals. We knew that we had to win to ensure qualification. If Spain beat European champions Denmark in Seville, a draw would be enough for us to get through. Northern Ireland had failed to qualify. One thing was certain, though: they could still stop us from going through if they managed to beat us the following evening.

With such high stakes, not to mention the hand of Irish history, the atmosphere was sure to be charged. But there was an extra edge. The match was taking place after a spate of Troubles killings. Three weeks previously, two IRA men had entered a fish and chip shop on Belfast's Shankill Road, intending to leave a bomb for a group of loyalist paramilitaries meeting upstairs. It exploded prematurely, blowing the bomber and nine other people in the chip shop to smithereens. Loyalist paramilitaries responded a week later, carrying out a wanton shooting at a pub in County Derry, killing eight. I remembered the news bulletin, which claimed that one of the gunmen had shouted 'trick of treat?' as he opened fire. Although I was playing my club football in England, the horror of the Troubles was only ever a newsreel away.

Tit for tat. 9-8? The grim tallies of the dead in both atrocities were close enough to seem like some sort of grotesque football score. The footballing authorities, understandably, were starting to become unnerved. There was talk of postponing the match, or playing it elsewhere – in Wembley or even in Rome. Then it was decided that the match would go ahead, as scheduled, at Windsor Park, Belfast. For security reasons we were instructed to fly the short distance back from Belfast to Dublin, which did little for everyone's nerves and wound Jack Charlton up no end. When the players were consulted we were all very brazen about actually playing the match; everyone had the attitude of 'let's just do it', and yet at the back of all our minds was creeping worry. Would athletes be targeted? Ha, ha! No way. Surely not. Shrug off the fear, lads, and move on.

However, in the days before the game someone mentioned the 1972 Olympics, when members of the Israeli Olympic team had been gunned down by the Palestinian group Black September. There was that momentary, stomach-tightening fear again. So, as the coach passed through the tight Belfast streets, past the red, white and blue kerb-stones and triumphal murals of King Billy on his horse, minds were racing with anxiety. Sitting in darkness, everyone was silent. I looked up and down the coach to the two special branch men, disguised in Football Association of Ireland tracksuits to blend in with us players. Even they seemed to be stroking their guns nervously.

As the coach drew up outside Windsor Park stadium, the escort of armoured cars started to pull away. I looked out of the window, first to the police helicopter still whirring noisily overhead and then to a set of five-a-side pitches illuminated by floodlights. I thought it was odd that they were empty; there should have been kids enjoying a kick-about. And then I saw the kids. Dozens of them, of all ages, from about ten to eighteen. They had spotted the coach and were converging on it. Undeterred by the police dogs bordering the stadium, this young mob crowded around the coach, making the gun sign with their hands. Every single one of them. With two fingers outstretched and their thumbs cocked, dozens of fingers rapped menacingly on the coach windows. "Fenian bastards!" Their lips pouted into a 'bang' as if they were pulling the trigger and blowing us away.

• • •

The fear that night in Belfast was more manageable because I was part of a band of brothers. Sure, the dark, silent final moments of that coach ride into the city were unnerving. But we dealt with the fear, as lads do, by cracking jokes. The hotel where we were staying before the game was out in the countryside, surrounded by a big golf course. Everywhere you looked, across the stunning grounds, there were Alsatians and policemen. Armoured cars patrolled up and down the drive and, of course, we had our armed plain clothes men in tracksuits masquerading as players. First we joked about whether Jack Charlton would, in his blustering and occasionally blundering way, accidentally put one of the special branch fellas in the starting line-up. Then, with black humour, we started speculating about who would be assassinated first. We all agreed that it would be the boss, Big Jack, and pretended to be relieved at this fact. Why Jack? Well, he was an easy target: a mountain of a man with ruddy cheeks, flat cap, a booming Geordie accent, and a purposeful stride. More importantly, though, he had a distinctively long neck. So long, in fact, that the players nicknamed him 'Swanny'. Don't worry, we joked, if anyone's going to take a bullet it'll be old swan neck.

What's more, the security concerns weren't going to put Jack off his pre-match ritual of leading the squad on a mid day stroll. On the day of the game, Jack and his assistant Maurice Setters were advised by the cops that walking the entire Republic of Ireland squad, all uniformed in tracksuits, around the leafy surrounds of the hotel was not a very good idea. But Jack would have none of it. So off we all set, behind Jack, accompanied by several policemen with semi-automatic weapons and an armoured car that trundled across the golf course tearing up the beautifully landscaped fairways with its dirty great tyre tracks. I can only imagine the groundsman's face when he saw the state of the 18th later that day.

Pre-match, at the hotel, there was another very funny moment. Jack Charlton was notorious for forgetting people's names. Before our final group game in the 1990 World Cup against the Netherlands, Jack had beseeched our captain Mick McCarthy to 'stay tight on Van Cleef'. Mick had to tell Jack that Lee Van Cleef was a dead Hollywood film star and not a Dutch striker. By those standards, Jack's name for me was fairly accurate: Alan McDonald. The problem was we were now playing Northern Ireland, who happened to be fielding a certain centre half named ... Alan McDonald. During the team talk I struggled to suppress my laughter as Jack told our team to watch out for Northern Ireland's centre half 'Alan McLoughlin' when they got a corner. As he continued to warn the team about the aerial threat of the opposition's Alan McLoughlin I could see Jack getting more and more annoyed with the smirk plastered across my face. 'And what the bloody hell is so funny?' he eventually asked. That was pure Jack.

• • •

All that seemed a world away in September 2012 as I was passed from Accident and Emergency to the Day Unit at Swindon Hospital. A young locum doctor came to see me. I told her about the pools of blood. She told me it was probably an infection or a kidney stone and gave me some painkillers. But as I drove home I felt more and more uneasy.

I'd been in my football kit all day so I headed for the shower. As I wearily opened the door a shot of pain made me bend double. I staggered into the shower cubicle but there was the pain again, this time worse. I am usually well able to deal with physical discomfort but I had to grope for the wall in order to steady myself. Minutes later, Deby found me writhing in agony on the bed, wrapped in my towel. She bundled me back into the car and sped back to the hospital.

When we got to A&E I refused to go into main reception and waited by the main door. I was a former professional footballer, a role model, healthy in body and mind. I did not want people to see me like this. I was doubled over and all but crying with the pain. They sent a wheelchair out for me and, as I was being wheeled in, a paramedic asked me 'out of ten, how bad is the pain?' I gritted my teeth. 'Eight or nine' I wheezed. Ten, more like.

• • •

As a professional footballer, you learn to deal with the pain of knocks and sprains and the more serious injuries. A terribly painful back injury eventually put paid to my playing days. Yet often, insults hurled at you from the crowd hurt more. I am thicker-skinned than most and little fazes me. But that night in November 1993 was different. Sitting on the substitutes' bench I heard every single word because there was no perspex glass behind us in the Windsor Park dug-out. I had never heard so many different expletives, and all accompanied by the words 'Taig' or 'Fenian'. There were threats on my life, my kids' lives, slurs about my mother, you name it. I just made sure not to turn round and make eye contact. Police forces on both sides of the border had urged fans to stay away but there were a few Republic of Ireland fans among the ten thousand or so spectators in that intense little ground. Those that were there must have been sitting on their hands. And who could blame them? If you're a Catholic, they say, Windsor Park can be about as welcoming as the ninth circle of hell.

Jack Charlton claimed he had never seen a more hostile atmosphere in all his playing or managing days, 'not even in Turkey'. Actually, I'm not so sure about that. Sitting on the bench in Istanbul in 1991 when Ireland's third goal went in, we found bags of piss raining down on us from the irate crowd, followed shortly thereafter by a dead cat. Minutes later, Jack turned to the substitutes and told us to warm up! For the one and only time, in unison we responded 'fuck off, Jack!' and, with one upward glance to the deceased feline splattered all over the Perspex above us and the thousands of Turks making slit-throat gestures behind, he consented. I'm not sure if Jack remembered that detail when recalling the hostility in Belfast, but I'll agree that Windsor Park that night was pretty nasty alright.

The atmosphere was not helped by Billy Bingham, the Northern Ireland manager, who had criticised what he called the Republic of Ireland's 'mercenaries'. He was referring to English-born players like me whom, he claimed, had chosen Ireland because 'they couldn't find a way of making it with England or Scotland'. That wound me up. Promising to reporters pre-match that the North would 'stuff us', Bingham made his way around the pitch before the kick-off, waving his arms to the fans, getting them stoked up. Oddly, though, by contrast to the 'mercenaries' slur, I regarded this act as mere gamesmanship; irresponsible perhaps, but more about pride, more of a football rivalry thing than a sectarian thing. Maybe I was just trying to impose the normality of competitive sport on a very abnormal situation by playing tricks on myself, trying to keep calm. Meanwhile, back on the bench, I was busy winding up our reserve goalie, and my close friend, Alan Kelly.

–'Oh my God!'

– 'What is it, Macca?'

– 'What's that?'

– 'What's what?'

– 'That little red spot on your forehead. I'm serious'

– 'What?'

– 'I think ... is it? ... Oh God, a red spot ... it's ... a sniper must have you in his sights!'

The dark humour was just our silly way of hiding the anxiety. Windsor Park that evening was a very strange place to be and the safest place was definitely on the pitch. For the rest of the match I shut out the abuse by engrossing myself in the game. Slowly, news started trickling through from Seville ... the Spanish goalie Zubizarreta had been sent off after only ten minutes. Surely Spain couldn't hold on against the Danes with only ten men?

But hold on the Spanish did and, better still, went 1-0 up after an hour. If Spain could protect their lead, a draw would be enough for us. With things going well in Seville, Jack decided we should push for the winner. On seventy minutes, and with the game still at 0-0, Jack signalled to Ray Houghton to come off and told me to get on the pitch, to pick up loose balls behind our front two men, and to do my damnedest to get us the winner. As I rose from the bench I could sense dozens of people in the stands behind me getting up too, with the sole intention of being able to hurl expletives at me more volubly. 'Keep calm, keep focused' I told myself. I removed my tracksuit, and busily tucked my shirt into my shorts. With the crowd spitting hatred at me, I stood on the touchline poised to enter the fray. Come on, ref! It seemed like an age before he stopped play and Ray trotted over. It was a blessed relief to leave that substitutes' bench and get on the pitch.

• • •

Little red spots... my physical agony had been signalled by that little red spot in the toilet bowl, a harbinger of the trauma to come. Back in Swindon hospital, I was given morphine for the pain and kept in overnight for observation and then a scan the next morning. In the night, though, I had to get up for a pee. And that's when the seriousness of my condition really hit me.

Try as I might, I could not pass fluid. I strained again and again. Still nothing. Then, a feeling of great relief as I finally passed something ... followed by horror at the colour and texture of it. I was passing blood again, but this time it was what I can only describe as pissing jam.

Later I was told that the jammy substances coming from my penis were blood clots. All night long, the jam kept coming. I was scared stiff. It was obvious that something was wrong, really wrong. I wanted to call Deby, to call my Mum and Dad, to share my anxiety. But if there's one thing I hate more than sympathy it's pity and so I grimaced and sweated in pain, alone, all night. When I looked down to my manhood and to the mess below, I wept. It was the stuff of nightmares.

• • •

Just after I came on that night in Belfast, Jimmy Quinn put Northern Ireland 1-0 ahead. It was a wonderful goal, a rifled volley. Packie Bonner had no chance of keeping it out. I knew Jimmy. When I'd signed for Swindon Town seven years previously (as a snot-nosed nineteen year old) Jimmy, an older pro, had taken me under his wing, regularly inviting me over for Sunday dinner with his family. But with that goal, my heart sunk. Defeat would put us out. I'd settled down to roast beef, gravy and spuds with that man. Now, as his teammates crowded around him in celebration, it looked like our American dream was over, killed by the avuncular Jimmy.

I looked back over to the bench, where Jack Charlton looked as if he was about to explode, kicking every ball, mouthing swear words, and flapping his arms around. Because I was on the pitch I was not aware until later of the famous altercation that had occurred after their goal. When Jimmy Quinn scored, Northern Ireland assistant manager Jimmy Nicholl had made sure to rub it in, shouting 'up yours!' to Maurice Setters. Shortly thereafter, as has gone down in the lore of that evening, Jack Charlton turned to Tony Cascarino and told him he was coming on. But Cass, being Cass, had left his jersey in the changing room. As he hurriedly unzipped his tracksuit, he was confronted by just a white cotton T-shirt. When Jack asked him what was taking him so long, Cass confessed his mistake and naively offered to play in his T-shirt instead of an official jersey. Jack was so angry I think he almost murdered him there and then. If something didn't change, and quick, our World Cup adventure would be over.

Then, minutes later, up the other end, we won a free kick for what looked to me like a fairly innocuous shoulder barge. Denis Irwin stood statuesque in the wind, ready to swing in one of his trademark free kicks with his right foot. I hovered on the edge of the box. Denis looped it quite deep into their box. As the ball was headed clear by a defender, I was there, loitering. I sensed Niall Quinn to my left, using his ample frame to obstruct Iain

Dowie and allow me space for a shot. Grateful to Quinny, I concentrated hard on the ball, thinking to myself that I needed to chest it down rather than snatch at it. In that killer moment, a calm came over me.

Momentarily, all the noise in the stadium disappeared. As the ball came to me, in my head I was back at Manchester United, the club that had signed me up as a sixteen year old. I was in the indoor gym with the shale pitch, the same pitch where my Dad's hero Georgie Best had trained, and where I had stayed on religiously after training every Tuesday and Thursday afternoon by myself, practising volleying the ball against the multi-coloured spots on the wall, painted on for target practice. I pictured the little red spot on the bottom left of the wall in United's indoor gym. 'Red spot, bottom left' I told myself. And with that target, that red spot, in my head, I let fly.

Sailing through a swarm of defenders, the shot swerved past Tommy Wright and into the bottom corner of the net. The Northern Ireland players, clad in dark green, seemed to collectively slouch as my smiling teammates in white and emerald sprinted to congratulate me. I wheeled away, fists pumping. It was the goal that would take Ireland to America. To USA '94. To the World Cup finals.

After the match, Paul McGrath asked me how I had been so cool with the finish. I had hit it so calmly and perfectly, said Paul, that I'd made the stress of the occasion disappear for him, to the extent that it almost felt like a Sunday league game when I'd scored. And so, like in a Sunday game, he slowly turned and trotted back to the half-way line after it went in, a new found calm about him. Well, the coolness of that finish came from the confidence of playing well all season. I was scoring goals week in, week out for Portsmouth and not long after that famous strike I went on to score a hat-trick against Blackburn Rovers (who would be crowned Premier League champions the following season) in an FA cup tie at Ewood Park.

OK, I know what you're thinking. I might have been in the form of my life, but scoring goals for an English First Division club does not equate to international prowess. I know I was an unlikely hero. In his latest book, journalist Eamon Dunphy called me 'the journeyman sub'. I had been a peripheral figure in Jack's squad, featuring only four times in the starting line-up in three years.

But in my appearances for Ireland I had also been unlucky: in fifteen games I had hit the bar twice, the post twice, and had two efforts cleared off the line. So I certainly wasn't as cool as the great Paul McGrath after I'd scored that evening. I clenched my fists and ran around screaming wildly for a few seconds. It wasn't the significance of the goal that made me react like that (our qualification still depended on Spain's result so we couldn't take anything for granted); no, it was relief and pent-up frustration pouring out. As I held my clenched fists towards my forehead, the overriding emotion was not 'we've qualified!' but 'thank God I've finally scored for my country!'

At the final whistle, more anxiety. Nobody had realised that the Spain versus Denmark match was still being played! An equaliser for the Danes against the ten-man Spanish would put them through in our stead. But somehow Spain held out. My goal had put us through.

Teammates smothered me in bear hugs: it seemed like Roy Keane would never let go of me; Packie Bonner just wrapped his big arms around me and kept whispering 'thanks, thanks' into my ear. In response to the earlier taunt, Big Jack approached Northern Ireland manager Billy Bingham at the final whistle and told him 'up yours too, Billy'. I think he later regretted it, but that encapsulated the poison of the evening. I didn't see this myself as I was on the pitch indulging the photographers, who were busy snapping the conquering hero. Arms aloft and smiling I gave my best pose for tomorrow's papers, the relief and exhilaration just oozing from me. Neither was it until much later that I saw the film The Road to America, which documented our qualifying campaign. The film crew were out and about in Dublin pubs soaking up all the angst surrounding this crunch match and in one, at half time, the reporter asked an anonymous young girl at the bar what should be done. She said to put on Alan McLoughlin and he would definitely get a goal. That woman, whoever she is, obviously possesses an admirable power to read the future and should be snapped up by Paddy Power immediately.

Predictably, Jack took the credit for the 'tactical masterstroke' of substituting me on. When the team got off the plane at Dublin airport, team captain Andy Townsend, Jack and me were interviewed by RTÉ. I said I'd been waiting for my breakthrough for a while and when the chance came I just hit it and it went in. Typically bland footballer interview, I suppose. At the subsequent press conference Jack, when asked about my strike, came up with a more memorable line: 'well, it justifies his existence for the last few years'.

Justifying my existence

'Justifies his existence'. Many a true word is uttered in jest and Jack's quip touched a raw nerve. Until that goal, I had spent a lot of my international career seeking justification. Continuously making the squad, coming off the bench to play for my country, but not scoring. I wasn't a striker, and I was usually only coming on for the last twenty or thirty minutes of each game, but I dearly wanted to break my duck with Ireland. So with that goal, I finally felt that my inclusion in Jack's Ireland squad was justified.

But when it came to justification, there was also a bigger issue at stake. With England failing to qualify for World Cup '94 some media voices were again questioning whether English-born players like me were justified in playing for Ireland at all.

Much of the nonsense about all that dates from when Ireland defeated England in Stuttgart in 1988 in the European championship. Ireland's goalscorer, Scottish-born Ray Houghton, had, as he put it, 'put the ball in the English net'. In saying that, he had also put a lot of people's backs up. The Irish football team under Jack Charlton subsequently came under heavy criticism for using the 'granny rule' – the FIFA stipulation that a grandparent's nationality qualified you to play for that country.

If Billy Bingham had called people like me 'mercenaries' for playing for Ireland others would say worse, much worse in the years to come. As an English-born Irishman, you're faced with a few identity crises to start with. Firstly, what do you call yourself? 'Anglo-Irishman' conjures up images of landed gentry on horses, which is fine if you come from that tradition, but I don't. Another alternative, 'Hiberno-English', just sounds pretentious. 'English-Irish' or 'Irish-English' is probably the least bad option but it's still clunky. So many of us just put up with the 'Plastic Paddy' label which is, at best, an unimaginative jibe. Then there's the music you're brought up with, which has the baddies – with their Cursed English Spleen – against the goodies – the Boys of the Old Brigade and the Bold Fenian Men. By virtue of birthplace and upbringing, you're in the former camp, but by virtue of parentage and tradition you're in the latter. Occasionally, there's a feelings of not being properly accepted by anyone: your accent marks you out in Ireland and your name marks you out in England. Next, of course, there's the context of the modern Troubles: the backdrop to my youth and that of many like me, which confused the identity issue further.

The fact is that both my parents are Irish-born. I didn't qualify under the much maligned 'granny rule'. I didn't need to. When my parents came to England they were both escaping an Ireland of insularity and unemployment. If it hadn't have been for economic and familial circumstances, I would have been Irish-born. And in the end, what bloody difference does it make? The business of nationalism is a strangely polarising place. A place of blacks and whites with very little room for grey. Take, for instance, Northern Ireland manager Billy Bingham questioning the right of us English-born Irishmen to play for the Republic. I looked across Windsor Park that evening and saw the numerous Union flags adorning the stands and at the people simultaneously yelling 'English bastard' and 'Fenian scum' at me while revelling in their own supposed Britishness. I just shrugged it off at the time. But when I think back, I find it ugly and a bit mad.

I could have played for England because I was born in Manchester, but instead I chose Ireland. I got the call up for both. Aged twenty-two, I got home to my house one day and there, on top of a pile of mail, was a pristine envelope with the three lions crest on it. My heart started racing. I had been selected to play for England 'B'. I excitedly started making telephone calls. I couldn't get through to Dad at his work, so next I called Mum. She was delighted with the news. Then I turned back to the pile of mail sitting on the door mat. Four other letters – fast food menu, council tax bill, energy bill – and one plain, slightly dog-eared brown envelope. It was from the Football Association of Ireland. I had been selected to play for Ireland 'B' too! I phoned Mum up again. This time, I heard a little crack of emotion in her voice as she told me how proud of me she was. Although she was trying to hide it, she was a lot more excited. This was the woman who had regularly cycled across Manchester in the rain just to watch me play school matches as a kid. And that was it for me: Ireland.

I was a professional footballer, not a crank. And so I was never bitter when it came to national identity, or confused about my national identity as an English-born Irishman. But it seems to have caused me some real aggro over the years nonetheless. I've stoutly defended the right of English-born Irishmen to play for Ireland ever since. Little did I expect one of my comrades on the pitch that evening in Belfast to join the naysayers in suggesting that I didn't appreciate the true value of playing for Ireland. But that's another story ...

• • •

Jack's remark about that goal justifying my existence was funny, but it also hurt. But then Jack never liked sharing the limelight. And it brought me back down to earth, so to speak. Nothing, though, brought me down to earth quite like passing great globules of blood from my penis. As a professional footballer you hold your head high, comfortable in the knowledge that you are physically fitter than the vast majority of people you come across in everyday life. Now I was rudely confronted with my own mortality and at the age of just forty-five. It set my mind racing in all sorts of frantic and gloomy directions.

A nurse came in to tell me that the doctor would be with me soon and swiftly pulled the curtain around the bed. I then heard the sound of the two patients with whom I was sharing the ward being wheeled out of the room. I knew this couldn't be good. Then, that horrible silence again.

Thirty seconds later a suave-looking doctor in a crumpled linen suit entered the room. He reminded me of the actor Don Johnson from the eighties cop show Miami Vice. He introduced himself as Dr J.W. Lacovou and he had the results of a scan I'd had earlier that day. He sat down on the bed beside me. This was another worrying sign.

– 'I'll come straight to the point, Mr McLoughlin, we've found a tumour in your right kidney.'

I put my hands over my face and started to shake my head; through my fingers, I looked at him again.

– 'Is it cancer?' I asked.

– 'Yes, in my mind, it is.'

– 'What do you mean, in your mind?' I responded.

– 'It's a cancerous tumour, Mr McLoughlin.'

The words hit me like a knockout blow. I felt dizzy and I swallowed hard, searching for words. This time there was no group of lads with me to act as a cushion to the fear. No one to banter with. No gang of fellow professional footballers to put their arms around me, to absorb the fear. I was all on my own.

– 'Can you take it out tomorrow?' I asked.

– 'No. I'm sorry. Another scan will take place in the morning. We can then decide what type of surgery it requires. It may take several weeks.'

The unspoken subtext was clear: they needed to determine whether or not the cancer had spread to other parts of my body. He placed his hand sympathetically on my lap.

– 'I'm sorry' I said.

He looked at me quizzically, as if I had stolen his line.

– 'No one's ever apologised to me at a moment like this before.'

– 'It's just ... it must be terrible having to break that sort of news to people'

He looked me in the eye.

– 'It is, Mr McLoughlin. It really is.'

2

From Old Trafford to Wembley

WHEN you are confronted with news like that, your world collapses. 'I'm a former professional footballer', I thought, 'I'm only forty-five, I'm young and I'm fit, this can't be happening to me'. But it was. It really was. And with that realisation, some of the grand organising concepts of life also fall to pieces. For instance, things like nationalism. The greatest moment of my career was undoubtedly scoring that goal in Belfast. Why? Because it got Ireland to the World Cup, yes; but also, I have to admit, because of the significance of scoring for the Republic versus Northern Ireland and for all the national-historical importance that entailed. After all, I was the first Republic of Ireland player ever to score against Northern Ireland on their home turf.

In 2012, though, with the cancer diagnosis, I thought a lot about death and started to wonder, among other things, 'what is a nation?' Many of those former arguments about how justified I was to play for Ireland now just seemed so awfully futile, so stupidly meaningless. My mortality was the headline act and all other concerns were mere bit players. Bodily function and malfunction eclipsed all else, occupying every conscious thought. Sleep came fitfully and, when it did, dreams occasionally and ever-so-sweetly sweetly drowned out the panic, only for my eyes to open again each waking day, for my brain to start working, and for the fear to set in.

When someone says that word to you – 'cancer' – the first

thought you have is fright and terror. It frightened me, of course. It frightened me more to tell my wife and my girls, my sister, and my friends. And it frightened me to tell my Mum and my Dad because, strangely, it felt as if, for the first time in my life, I had let them down.

Whenever I needed to justify my right to play for Ireland, or just about anything else for that matter, all I had to do was to look to Mum and Dad. Mum is from Knockaderry in County Limerick. Dad is from Largan, between Headford and Tuam, on the Galway / Mayo border. Both are kind, loving, genuine, hard-working and honest. My parents were both in their early twenties when they emigrated. Like many other young people in the Ireland of their generation, they moved to England for work and for the dream of a better life. The Ireland they left was no place for young people. Work was scarce; life was hard; social, economic and cultural opportunities drastically limited. Aided by legions of self-appointed moral guardians, the bishops' diktats held inordinate political sway. The thwack of the crozier could never subdue the charm of rural Ireland. But along with Ireland's poverty, dislocation and insularity, the national atmosphere stifled youthful ambition. And so Ireland lost my Mum and Dad and hundreds of thousands like them. Both, separately, crammed onto the cattle boat in Dublin and jostled off it when it docked in Holyhead. Both eventually ended up in Manchester, where Mum found a job in the Dunlop factory and Dad worked in the building trade. They met one another quite by chance, when they sat together on a bus one rainy Sixties afternoon and got chatting.

The thought of Mum and Dad meeting like that is an enduringly romantic image for me. Whenever I think of it, it plays out like a black and white movie. My parents are the protagonists in the love story, their eyes lighting up at the sight of one another, flanked by grey-looking commuters with their heads buried in newspapers. For these two young emigrants from the west of Ireland, the romance of that first meeting helped to quell uncomfortable memories of life back home.

Mum's mother, my maternal grandmother, was Limerick woman Bridget Doherty. Born in 1902 in Tournafulla, she married my grandfather, Michael Moran, in 1928. In her sixties, she moved to Manchester shortly after my Mum. Her marriage to Michael had broken down irreparably, despite her patient efforts. Four of her five siblings had settled in Manchester by that point and so, with tears rolling down her cheeks, one morning she quietly packed her things and followed them over the water. It was a heart-rending decision for a middle-aged woman to make. In Ireland at that time marital breakdown brought with it great stigma. In taking the decision to leave my grandfather she knew that returning to Ireland was out of the question. A devout Catholic and daily communicant, Nan lived to be ninety-eight and died in the year 2000, safe in the knowledge that she was going to a better place. I used to listen attentively to her stories about the hated Black and Tans, whom she'd encountered as a teenage girl during the War of Independence. Even as a child, I was awed by the sorrow and resilience that had so clearly marked her life.

And what about my surname: McLoughlin? Well, Dad's mother, Anne Reilly, met Joseph McLoughlin (a Longford man) while working in Tuam and they were married there in 1942. They had two sons, of whom Dad was the eldest, and one daughter. Joseph needed to provide for his family and so, after he had found work in England, the family followed him to Manchester, in search of work and new opportunities.

Unfortunately, the move did not prove a happy one and Joseph eventually relocated to Scotland, where he began a new life. Anne, my Gran, stayed put in Manchester with the children. And so I would not meet Joseph, my grandfather, until his former wife Anne's funeral in 1992, when I was aged twenty-five and where, against my instincts and only at my Dad's request, I shook his hand.

For all these reasons, we did not return to Ireland that often when I was a child. When we did go back home, it would be with Mum's brother, uncle Pat. I learned to hurl with him, knocking a sliotar around the local Gaelic pitches in Limerick, but most of the time we played football (soccer) together. Mum and Dad were married in Manchester in 1965. Sadly, more family tragedy was lurking around the corner. Their first born child, my older sister Patricia, died aged only fourteen months, of a hole in her heart and other complications. The death of their baby at such a tender age brought my parents huge sadness. It's the sort of grief which is difficult for anyone who hasn't lost a child to get their head around. When Patricia died, Mum was already heavily pregnant with me and she gave birth to me at Withington Hospital, Manchester, on 20 April 1967. I was born just six weeks after Patricia died. It must have been a heart-rending time for Mum and Dad.

Closet Red

Manchester in the Seventies. Growing up in that city at that time, football took precedence above all else. Mum and Dad had one more child after me: my younger sister, Diane, who is eighteen months younger than me, and whose passion was Irish dancing. But football seemed to place all other concerns in its shade. For starters, we had a whopping great football stadium on our doorstep. We lived at 162 Maine Road, right next to Manchester City's ground. One of my earliest memories is sitting at the window of our terraced house, suffering from the mumps, looking really sorry for myself, a blanket wrapped around me, and some City fans, on their way to the match, pointing at me and laughing. Was that where my lack of time for pity and sympathy began? With bigger boys taking the piss? With that Mancunian attitude that no one is that precious, that you take life's blows on the chin and move on? Perhaps.

City's training ground was just five hundred yards from our front door and, as a kid, I would regularly walk up there to watch stars like Joe Corrigan and Peter Barnes knocking the ball around. Eventually, the City players grew used to me and would say 'hello' and ruffle my hair as they walked past. While Joe Corrigan was the friendliest of the players, I identified most with City's Scottish midfielder Asa Hartford. Because my younger sister Patricia had died of a heart condition while still a baby, Hartford's story resonated with me. Famously, in 1971 his big money move to Leeds United was scuppered by the late discovery of an underlying heart condition. He played on regardless with a grit and determination that seemed to defy Leeds United's doctors and their dark diagnosis. I soon decided that if I had a son, I'd call him Asa. Sometimes, on a Saturday afternoon, I'd go to Maine Road watch the same players from the stands. Getting into the ground early, I would perch myself on the wall between the Kippax Stand and the North Stand, thus ensuring I got a proper view of Peter Barnes mesmerising hapless full backs with his dancing feet and Hartford almost effortlessly dispossessing the opposition midfield.

Dad often took me matches, but I was standing on my own on the afternoon when I started to really appreciate how beautiful the father-son relationship can be. One afternoon in the Kippax, I was surprised to find a tall, immaculately attired black man standing beside me. When the City goalie, Alex Williams, made a fairly routine early save this suave-looking guy, hitherto demure in his shirt and tie and hat, started celebrating animatedly, as if he'd just won the football pools. I surveyed him quizzically. Turning to me, he enthusiastically put his arm around my shoulder and pointed at Williams – one of the first black goalkeepers to play at the top level in England – 'Come here, kid. See the goalie?' he excitedly exclaimed, 'that's my son!' I looked at the pride etched across his face and resolved that I would do my best to create the same emotion for my Dad one day.

There was a big problem though: we lived deep in blue territory and I regularly watched City play at home, but all my family, me included, were Manchester United fans. Dad took me to see my first United game when I was aged only four, so I could see the great George Best – his hero – and his unique footballing style. From that point on, I was hooked on United. Early on, then, located deep within Manchester City territory, I was forced to settle into a life of being a closet Manchester United fan. This was some predicament.

The fierceness of the Manchester derbies of the 1970s aggravated my situation. There were several memorable clashes characterised by hard, mouthy northern men indulging in gamesmanship and biting tackles. BBC commentators lamented the bad example such ungentlemanly conduct was setting to the youth. As a young kid, though, I was spellbound by the theatricality of these classic games. In one, City's stocky Franny Lee was so convinced that George Best was play-acting that he melodramatically flung himself into the mud beneath the referee's feet. In another, a player from each side received a red card only for both men to refuse to leave the pitch, plunging proceedings into anarchy. The United player in question was one of my future managers, the fiery Scottish-Italian Lou Macari. Violence on the terraces was never far away, either. The away fans would be herded into the top right hand corner of Maine Road's Kippax Stand and fights would regularly break out. Dad would not let me go to Manchester derby matches as they were too dangerous but, aged twelve, I found myself in the middle of a huge brawl between City fans and visiting Liverpool supporters. Fists flew in every direction and, as bodies surged and the police waded in, I found myself crushed and gasping for breath. Starting to panic, I hit the floor and crawled away, clutching on to people's ankles as I did so. I later emerged from underneath a turnstile: unscathed, scared, and just a little bit excited.

If the nastiness between red and blue was ever getting too much, there was always the green. There was no Catholic school nearby our house, so I attended Saint Ambrose's Catholic primary school, which was a bus ride away. At Saint Ambrose's, my first football team was the Cub Scouts. Dad wasn't too happy about me joining the Scouts, but Mum overruled him. If she could get off work, she would cycle long distances across the city to watch me play away matches with the school team. If Dad could get time off work, he'd come and watch too. I also played for my secondary school, Saint Mark's Catholic secondary school, Didsbury (now Barlow High) and was selected for Manchester Boys in all age groups throughout my primary and secondary schooling. My school, Saint Mark's, was two bus journeys or a twenty minute cycle away from Maine Road. But it was important to Mum and Dad that I went to a Catholic school, so we upped sticks to Didsbury. That was how I ended up in Saint Mark's, sitting alongside a rebellious young kid named Gallagher.

I soon learned that there was a seniority at Saint Mark's based on the name of the place. The brightest pupils were placed in class 'M'. The next brightest were in 'A', and so on with 'R' and 'K', with those kids who were struggling the most placed in the bottom class: 'S'. I remember being disappointed that I'd ended up in 'S' class along with all the problem kids. So was Mum. She'd confessed her worries about my school progress to one of the teachers at my previous school, Mr Sudlow, whom she met while out shopping in Manchester one day. Sudlow who, on more than one occasion, had looked up from his piles of marking to see me enthusiastically charging around the playing field after a football, sought to reassure her. 'Don't worry, Mrs McLoughlin, he'll be a footballer one day'. Though well intended, I don't think this went down too well with my anxious mother.

One of my fellow stragglers in 'S' class at Saint Mark's was the Gallagher lad, Noel, later to form Oasis with younger brother Liam, and similarly football-mad. In fact, while there was every indication that Noel was a Manchester City fanatic, there was little indication that he would make a career for himself in music. Noel, like me, was into Paul Weller and The Jam and had the haircut and the fishtail parker jacket to prove it (Mum and Dad would never let me have the mod look). But Noel didn't excel in music classes. If the poor old music teacher at Saint Mark's, a patient black man named Mr Noon, had to put up with me murdering 'Three Blind Mice' on the recorder for my O-Level practical exam, Noel's efforts, I recall, really weren't that much better.

When Oasis were in their pomp, Noel famously sported a

Union Jack guitar, catching the mood of the Britpop era of the 1990s. But, like me, Noel was of Irish Catholic stock. My parents moved north across the city from West Didsbury to Fallowfield when I was thirteen. There, local Irish identity was cemented by Saint Kentigern's Church Fallowfield Catholic social club (St Kent's) which was opposite my house, and which was the only place we could go for a pint and a game of pool when we were teenagers below the legal drinking age. Instead of music, all my socialising with Noel took place around football. Noel, of course, was a diehard City fan, and he would often walk from Burnage, where he lived, to Maine Road stadium where we'd watch matches together with two or three other lads from school. I had some time for City, but little did Noel or the others realise that I was secretly a United fan; I don't think they would have taken the news that well.

Like Noel and all the other kids I grew up with, I always wanted to be a professional footballer. But the prevailing wisdom was that I was too small. As I progressed through secondary school, playing for Manchester Boys, a lot of my mates started to get games in the youth teams of local clubs like Stockport, Bury, Bolton, and even City or United. And yet I was overlooked because I was deemed too diminutive. Because of my short stature and slight build I was never picked to play for the county of Lancashire or Lancashire Boys, which would have meant stepping up a level.

I was very upset about this, resentful in fact. After all, Diego Maradona, at five foot five, was the greatest player on earth at that time. Then, midway through my final year in secondary school, I heard that a local team, Chadderton (which is near Oldham) were playing two games against Manchester United's youth team over a two week period. This was my chance. I might have been an 'S' class straggler, but I had no problem putting together a cunning plan to get spotted by United. My friend at the time, Johnny Young, was playing for Chadderton and so I made sure to hang out with him a bit more than usual, to give my all in kickabouts so that he was in no doubt about how good I was. Endorsed by Johnny, it wasn't long before I was turning up to train with Chadderton and managed to cajole my way onto the team, to the great annoyance of a few people in their set-up. I was quite single-minded, though: at fifteen, I knew that this was the last chance I would get to make it as a professional footballer. I was playing for my future. The manager of Chadderton knew immediately what I was up to and, taking dim view of my opportunistic ambition, only played me for the last twenty minutes of the first game. Luckily, however, one of their regular players fell ill before the second match, and I played the full ninety minutes in the return fixture. That game was played at The Cliff, Manchester United's training ground.

After that second game my parents, who'd come to watch, had some incredible news for me. Eric Harrison, the Manchester United youth team coach who would later be credited with producing 'Fergie's fledglings', had approached Mum and Dad by the side of the pitch. Eric had been ghosting his way through the crowd, making discreet enquiries about who the lad wearing number four for Chadderton was, and where his parents were standing. Finding my parents, he briefly introduced himself before instructing them to bring me in to United the following Thursday night to train with the youth team. And then, like an apparition, he was gone.

When Mum and Dad told me, I could hardly believe what I was hearing. I was exhilarated. At first I thought it was a joke. My Dad was aware of my cunning plan to get spotted and I half thought he was winding me up. Dad never played cruel jokes like that; it was just that the enormity of the news, to a teenager, was almost too much to take in. My parents lavished me with hugs and congratulations. Having watched United play for years alongside my Dad, whether on the telly or, initially, while perched on his shoulders at Old Trafford, this was an extraordinary affirmation of the father-son relationship. And Mum, too, was delighted; she had been my ever-present on the touchline, leaning on her bicycle, mouthing words of calm encouragement to me while wannabe-football manager fathers all around her bawled obscenities at the twenty-boy swarm converging on a lump of leather like stray dogs over a bone. What's more, now I had been picked to play for them, I could finally also step out of the closet and admit to supporting Manchester United!

After the good news, I had three months to make an impression and try and secure an apprenticeship. So I worked my bollocks off, staying behind long after everyone else had left training to practice on my own. My efforts must have further impressed Eric Harrison for, aged fifteen, I got the very last apprenticeship handed out by Manchester United.

There was an extra significance to winning that apprenticeship. On the very same day it was awarded to me, seventeen years previously, my older sister Patricia had died aged just fourteen months. My winning the apprenticeship was some good news for Mum and Dad, who would have done anything for me and my younger sister, Diane. Diane was an excellent Irish dancer and danced for the Lomax school of Irish Dancing in Manchester. Mum and Dad devoted as much time to Diane's dancing as my football and I had to sit at many a Feis over the years. They even tried to get me to dance, but it was a non-starter for me, as my wife Deby will attest. Likewise, they devoted time and effort to helping me fulfil my dream of becoming a footballer. A few months earlier Dad had bought me a pair of Puma S.P.A. Kings. They were the best boot on the market at the time, were made of kangaroo leather, and had cost him a week's wages.

My Dad earned his money with his hands and so knew exactly the back-breaking work that a week's wages equated to. He and Uncle Martin had set up a small building company and, over the summer months, I would go labouring with them to earn a few quid. The work was brisk and the graft was hard. I would spend the days mixing concrete or wheeling a wheel barrow filled to overflowing around the site. By the end of the day, I'd be sweating, exhausted and cursing the blisters on my hands. Dad, surveying me, would say 'do you want to do this for the rest of your life Alan?' 'Grafting day in, day out? My answer was always 'no, I want to be a professional footballer'. 'Then you must work for it' Dad and uncle Martin would reply. These two men punished their bodies in order to provide for their families and taught me that hard work and persistence would pay off if you grafted for it. It was a life lesson which is still with me today and one which I have passed onto my daughters Abby and Megan. That's why, back in 1983, a tear in my eye, breaking the good news to Mum and Dad meant so much. Securing that Manchester United apprenticeship, I felt, had at long last justified their love and faith in me.

United apprentice

No sooner had the exhilaration at getting into United arrived, it was almost eradicated by poor health. Weeks before I was due to take my school exams and go on to join Man United as an apprentice, I was struck down by a mystery illness. It was my first adult experience of serious illness and, of course, not the last. My teenage affliction rudely sapped me of all my strength and confined me to a lengthy stay in bed. For a sixteen-year-old, going from peak physical fitness to being bed ridden was agonising. More worryingly, I could not stop vomiting. Mum called a doctor to the house. When he recommended to my anxious parents that I be brought to hospital to undergo an X-ray, they tried hard to conceal their worry. The results showed a shadow on one of my lungs. I was scared. The continuous throwing up was bad enough; the shadow on the lung even worse; but the thought of having my life's dreams stolen from me in such an untimely manner was utterly shattering.

It was no good: Manchester United had to be informed. My parents spoke to the club about my mystery affliction, my symptoms, and the results of the X-ray. The club doctors responded with a robust remedy. They gave Mum an extra £25 a week, instructing her to buy Guinness and steak with the money. This diet, they promised, would strengthen me up. Twenty-five quid was more than enough to buy the choicest, juiciest steak and more Guinness than was good for a teenager. I soon took to the new regimen with all the relish of a plump food critic, drinking two pints or so of Guinness a day and chomping my way through lots and lots of steak. Slowly but surely my strength returned; the vomiting ceased; and I again dared to dream that I could make it as a professional footballer.

The illness had set me back, though, and I still wasn't one hundred per cent physically fit when I reported to Old Trafford for my first training session. That first session was intimidating psychologically, too. Because I had joined United through the back door, I knew none of the top schoolboy players who I was now thrown together with. And so the chatter and the banter amongst these talented young players, bred from years of familiarity, largely bypassed me. Everyone boarded the minibuses: the first team in one, the youth team in another. We piled out at Heaton Park where United manager Big Ron Atkinson started yelling instructions at us.

– 'See that tree over there?' Ron shouted to his players, who were hopping out of the minibuses like troops from a helicopter.

– 'Yes, gaffer.'

– 'Run there and back. Now! Don't be last!'

By today's standards the training was crude: no sports science techniques, no heart rate monitors; merely hard work, and plenty of it. Running. Running. Then more running. After sprinting to the first tree and back we then moved on to the next tree, and so on, with the distances getting further and further. You couldn't be seen to be weak and, in my condition, it hit me like a ton of bricks.

Shadowing the burly Ron was United's youth team supremo, Eric Harrison. Eric was an imposing Yorkshireman who filled me with terror but taught me everything I know about football. Following his playing career, he'd ended up coaching at Everton. He was brought into United by Ron, his old mate from the armed services, and was kept on by Alex Ferguson when he took over at Old Trafford. Eric, as many have acknowledged, was the real mastermind behind the brilliant young team that emerged at Manchester United under Fergie. It was Eric that had first given a break to players like Mark Hughes, Norman Whiteside, David Beckham, Ryan Giggs, Paul Scholes, Nicky Butt and the Neville brothers. He inspired a terrific sense of passion, perseverance, endeavour and loyalty in his young players. And mental strength.

The reason I was the last player to receive a United apprenticeship was the Thatcher government's introduction of the Youth Training Scheme (YTS), which replaced apprenticeships. On the day when United received their first YTS recruits, an ITN news crew turned up at training to report on how the scheme was being implemented at a top football club. That morning, Eric was on his best behaviour, indulging the film crew and allowing his young players to be interviewed. As soon as the news team had left, his attitude changed. Now we were off camera, he instructed one of our number to stand on the goal-line and the rest of us, in turn, to smash the ball at him. This continued until everyone had taken their turn to have balls walloped at them. Would you flinch? Would you duck out of the way of the ball? Or, would you take the ball full-on in the chest, the side of the head, or the bollocks? Would you absorb the pain and carry on? Of course we were technically gifted, we were at Manchester United. Eric wanted more than that: he wanted mentally strong characters. Years later, during a televised Portsmouth game, I was standing in the wall facing a free kick which was flying straight at my head. As the ball hurtled towards my nose I remember thinking 'this is going to hurt' followed instantly by the thought 'don't flinch, Eric might be watching'. That was the extent of the loyalty: by that point I was thirty years old, for Christ's sake!

Eric's regime at The Cliff was legendarily intense. It had to be. Back in those days, the youth team would line up against the first team once a week, and we had to be able to hold our own. All of United's teams, from the youths up, trained at The Cliff. It was too small, really, but it meant that I regularly played alongside the older players. My jaw dropped in awe when in the presence of England captain Bryan Robson. Big Ron Atkinson broke the British transfer record in bringing Robson to United in 1981 for one-and-a-half million pounds, a record which was still standing when I was at Old Trafford. Watching him train, I thought he was worth every penny and then some. Some of my fellow youth players resented the task of cleaning the older professionals' footwear, but I took to cleaning Bryan Robson's New Balance boots with vigour. He had a great style and elegance and seeing him lift the FA Cup for United in 1983 and 1985 cemented his hero status for me. One of the most impressive things about Robbo was his successful overcoming of serious and persistent injury problems on his way to his place at the top of the game. Early on, I decided to emulate that steel and determination in the face of physical set-backs as best I could.

Big Ron was given a big wallet by United's board and for youth team players like me this meant the chance to rub shoulders with some big-money, big-talent players. More than just cleaning their boots, after our match against the first team each week older players like Ray Wilkins or Gordon Strachan would put their arm around you and offer you encouragement. Then there were those inspirations, like Mark Hughes and Norman Whiteside, that Ron had blooded as youngsters and who had made the grade. Promising apprentices like me would sometimes get the chance to cross balls for these exalted characters at training. As a sixteen year old it was a proud feeling when, after whipping a ball into the box, I'd see Robson, the England captain and my hero, rise up and nod it into the net. Most importantly, it instilled an emboldening pride and confidence in me at a tender age.

Playing against the first team was another privilege. Peter Barnes, who I'd watched from the stands at Maine Road and was now playing for United, recognised me as the scrawny kid who'd turn up day-in, day-out to watch him and his City teammates train. Wiping his mop of fair hair from his eyes, he shook my hand. I wasn't expecting what he said next: 'now listen, lad, you'll be marking me today, so let me beat you a few times.' Of course I thought about it for a moment. He might have been getting on a bit, but this was the great Peter Barnes, after all. As soon as Barnes had walked away from me, however, Eric Harrison – who'd been watching like a hawk – was at my shoulder.

– 'What did he say to you?' he demanded.

– 'Err. He just asked me if I would let him take it round me a couple of times' I answered.

– 'And what did you say?'

I looked at Eric and shrugged my shoulders. He stared back, unimpressed.

'If he bloody well goes past you once – just once – I will kick your arse. Understand?'

I did not need to be told twice. Under Harrison's tutelage, I captained Manchester United Youth for two years. With Eric it was all about getting young players to handle pressure. When playing for United Reserves, we played Lancashire league matches against Liverpool teams like Everton, South Liverpool, Liverpool and Barrow, not to mention Man City. I was a full back and sometime midfielder but, despite the fact that I'm five foot nine and a half, Eric often played me at centre half. Before my first match as captain, against Arsenal Youth, Eric was making his way down the team coach. 'Who's going to be captain today, Eric?' I asked cockily. 'I'm not sure yet, Alan' he replied. 'Well, I'd like to be' I snapped back. And so Eric made me captain. It turned out to be a mixed blessing. That day I had to mark my future Irish teammate Niall Quinn

– all six foot four of him. I didn't win too many headers that day.

The Manchester United first team manager, Big Ron Atkinson, was a flamboyant, larger-than-life character who imbued the club with his inimitable sparkle. A former player himself, Ron used to love joining in with training matches, throwing his plump frame about the pitch with his players. Perma-tanned and almost bursting out of his tight shorts, he'd bound down the little slope between the changing rooms and the pitches and get stuck in. On one such occasion, I went to tackle him but stumbled and he glided past me with ease. 'Sod this', I thought, as Ron, full of himself, went on a slow mazy dribble, and so I slid in at him from behind, winning the ball, but sending him flying into a big muddy puddle beside the pitch. Seeing Ron flounder in the puddle sent the canteen staff and injured players, watching from the windows of the training complex, into raptures of laughter. The players burst out laughing too. That did not put me in Ron's good books.

It was at United, while rubbing shoulders with first team players, that I first met another future Irish teammate, Paul McGrath, who was a few years older than me. Paul, like Mark Hughes, was quiet; but he was an imperious player and, with his big afro, really stood out. For all his gentleness, it was obvious from the outset that alcohol was an issue with Paul. On one occasion we were being put through some punishing sprints on United's shale training pitch, a session of 'every line and back' which involved dashes to the six yard box, then the eighteen yard box, then the half way line, then eighteen, six yard, and top line. Paul, struggling to work off the booze from the night before, collapsed half way through and, on his hands and knees, started throwing up. There were plenty of other players in the United set up who were heavy boozers; Bryan Robson was one, but he was a great trainer, even after knocking back ten pints the night before.

I played over forty games for United Reserves but, ultimately, there were just too many established players ahead of me. My best chance of a breakthrough was at full back, but with the likes of Clayton Blackmore and internationals like Arthur Albiston and Mike Duxbury performing strongly in that position, I didn't get a look in, and the furthest I got at United was the Reserves. Finally, after three years with United – two as an apprentice and one on a professional contract – Big Ron let me go. It was early May 1986. Things were already starting to unravel for Atkinson, who had struggled to replace his midfield fulcrum Ray Wilkins after he left for AC Milan in 1984. Although the club won the FA Cup again in 1985, the departure of Mark Hughes to Barcelona was a further sign that Ron was on borrowed time. I was at United long enough to remember the whispers going round the club that Aberdeen manager Alex Ferguson was waiting in the wings. I suppose that I was of little concern to Big Ron as he struggled with bigger problems. In the greater scheme of things, letting young Alan McLoughlin go was no big deal. For me, however, it was devastating.

Following the Bradford stadium disaster and the Heysel disaster the year before, football was in a bad place. And so was I. Having just turned nineteen, and for the first time in my life, I experienced the sort of disappointment that is so crushing you can almost taste it.

Where's Swindon?

United's decision to let me leave was, I'm told, a narrow one. Out of four senior coaches, all needed to unanimously agree to keep a player. I received three votes out of four. Eric Harrison, who'd voted to keep me, told me he was disappointed with the decision and I could tell that he meant it. He also told me to keep my head up and to not give up on my dream and, through Eric's intercession, days later, I found myself thrown into the Stoke City reserve team, heading to northern France for an end of season friendly tournament which also featured Oldham Athletic and two French sides. The footballing adventure would continue if I could prove my worth to Stoke City. Or so I thought.

The tournament itself was one of those odd pre-season affairs but for me it was a stage. Once again, I played as if my life depended on it and won the player of the tournament award. Now, I thought, it was certain that I would get another chance at making it as a professional footballer. On the way back, at Hilton services on the M6, the Stoke youth team manager, Tony Lacey, made his way down the coach. I was sitting at the back of the bus and, watching Lacey's demeanour as he walked down the aisle, sensed that he had broken bad news to some of the other young lads. If anything, this made me sure that it was good news for me, the player of the tournament. Apart from playing alongside them, I didn't know these other hopefuls. They were, one-by-one, having their egos and dreams punctured by Lacey, his hand lingering on a shoulder before moving on to the next unlucky candidate. Surely I would be the exception. After all, I was the Manchester United recruit. How many of these other lads had trained alongside Bryan Robson? I felt a shock of nervous, upbeat excitement pulse through me as Lacey turned, finally, to me.

– 'Alan'

– 'Yes, Tony'

– 'I'm sorry, Alan, we have lots of players at the club in your position and we don't see you as an option at Stoke.'

– 'What?'

– 'You were the best player out there, but I'm afraid that we aren't taking on any of you young lads.'

And then I saw through the whole thing. The young hopefuls, myself included, had been drafted in so that Stoke City could fulfil their commitment to an unimportant end of season tournament. In doing so, they'd obviously been able to give their younger professionals a rest after the long league campaign. None of us had a chance of being taken on. The dice were loaded from the start. My face turned red as the emotion of it all overcame me. I thought of Stoke City's younger professionals sunning themselves on a beach somewhere. Then I thought of Dad, slaving away to buy me the Puma SPA boots made of bloody kangaroo skin; of all the hard work I'd put in at United; of all that I'd sweated in the French tournament for a futile cause.

'You're fucking shit!' I bellowed at Lacey. He looked completely taken aback. At that point Joe Royle, the Oldham Athletic manager, sitting at the top of the coach, swivelled round in his seat. 'Keep your voice down, young man!' he demanded.

'And you can fuck off as well!' I yelled back.

As the coach made its way back up north, storm clouds swirled above my head. Never mind Lacey; Royle was an Everton, Man City and England legend and I mulled over having told a footballing titan to fuck off. I had been raised a decent Catholic and Mum and Dad would have been horrified by my attitude. But they'd also raised me to possess a keen sense of justice and a too-the-point nature. I decided that I was still justifiably angry – for the other kids as much as me – about how we had been used on the French trip. I stayed on the coach until it reached Oldham. As I passed Joe Royle on the way out, he shot me a nasty glare. I apologised to him for swearing. He acknowledged me with a barely audible grunt. Then, still pumping with adrenalin, I asked him 'Can I come to Oldham on trial, Joe?' He looked back at me as if unable to believe my cheek. 'I'll think about it' was all he said.

Thereafter, four weeks of footballing limbo. A holiday in Spain with a mate did nothing to dispel the nagging feeling. Then, the last resort of the young footballing desperado, an exit trial: a massive free-for-all for all the young players released by their clubs that year. From this last-chance saloon, a jamboree of hundreds of young players, would emerge a handful offered trials with professional clubs. For the vast majority, though, no news would mean bad news; the lack of a subsequent phone call meaning professional football was over as an option and it was time to start looking for a 'real' job.

I travelled up to the exit trial, which was at Durham University, with Dad. Lads and dads huddled around before the parents were separated from the triallists, who crammed into the far-too-small changing rooms to await instruction in awkward silence. Every time there was a noise from the corridor or the door opened, young faces turned expectantly and in unison, only for another silent triallist to shuffle his way in. Finally, word got round that the scouts had arrived and, finally, we were given kits and separated into several teams. Trying to prove my worth proved almost impossible. Each young man, going through his own heartache, was very much focused on his own game. No one wanted to make friends. No one wanted to pass the ball. All anyone wanted to do was to keep possession, hoping to look good and draw the attention of a scout from a professional club who might be watching from the sidelines among the throngs of equally desperate parents. On the way home we stopped at Scotch Corner service station for a cup of tea. It felt like this really was make or break. If I didn't receive a phone call after the exit trial, that was that. I didn't say so and neither did Dad. We didn't need to. We both knew it.

Four weeks of waiting beside the phone in Mum and Dad's house. Four weeks of stroppy impatience. And then, one day, out of the blue, the phone rang. It was Lou Macari, the former Manchester United and Celtic footballer, and now manager of newly promoted Division Three side Swindon Town.

– 'Hello. Am I speaking with Alan?'

– 'Yes.'

– 'Hello Alan, it's Lou Macari. I want you to come down to Swindon for a month's trial.'

My response was instantaneous.

– 'Errrmm ... where's Swindon?'

– 'It's in Wiltshire.'

I thought about this for a second, and then asked:

– 'Errrmm ... Where's Wiltshire?'

OK, my Saint Mark's 'S' class English geography might not have been the best, but I told Lou I was willing. The next day, as my parents prepared for the long drive, the phone rang again. This time it was Joe Royle's secretary at Oldham Athletic. Joe must have remembered me after all. Oldham was a more attractive option for me because, being a Manchester lad, at least I knew where it was, but they wanted to offer me a one week trial only whereas, at Swindon, I'd have a month to prove myself. So after politely declining Oldham me, Mum, and Dad set off instead for Wiltshire, wherever that was. Before we left Manchester, we called into

Dad's brother uncle Martin, his wife – my aunty Mary – and my Nan, who lived with them. We lived only twelve doors apart and I was always in their house, playing with my cousins, and basking in the love and affection of my extended Irish family. We are a very emotional family and I would cry at Lassie Come Home, let alone the scene in Bambi where his mother is shot, so my collar was wet with tears as I waved them all goodbye from the window of Dad's red Toyota van.

Down the motorway, through Birmingham and the Midlands and, hours later, into Wiltshire. When we arrived at Swindon's County Ground it was late and there was no one there. The only person around was Chris Scott, a stalwart of the Swindon set-up. He called Lou Macari, who came to collect me. I hugged Mum and Dad goodbye and waved as my Dad's van disappeared from sight, making its slow way back to Manchester, swallowing the slight lump in my throat, and hoping that Lou didn't notice.

Since I didn't even know where Swindon was, I knew no one in the town. I spent my first restless night in digs beside the ground, in an uncomfortable bunk bed. The mattress had more lumps than the Himalayas and I didn't get much sleep. I got up early the next day, still full of tingling anticipation. The one professional at the club I knew was goalkeeper Fraser Digby, whom I met the next day. I'd spent three years with Fraser at Man United and he'd moved to Swindon three months before me. Fraser had his kit on, which I thought was odd given that it was the close-season. It soon became clear that it was club photo day and so, with everyone else kitted out, I stayed in the changing room on my own. Minutes later, manager Lou Macari popped his head around the door. 'Get some kit on!' he told me. 'But I thought I was only here for a month's trial!' I thought to myself as I undressed. Later I found out that Lou was always going to sign me but that he was keeping me on tenterhooks for a month to see how I would react. Mind games. Typical Lou Macari, as I would discover.

Lou Macari liked to test you like that, to challenge you. I was easy prey, I suppose, because I was a teenager a long way from home, and he soon took me under his wing as 'Little Al'. I had played alongside Lou at Manchester United in the twilight of his career, when he was an established professional and very much the joker of the pack. As a manager, though, he was a disciplinarian and a real stickler for fitness. He would put the squad through a punishing five and a half mile run every Thursday and, as a teetotaller, would not tolerate any of his players drinking or smoking. To make sure he was obeyed, he had instructed all the landlords in Swindon to inform him if they saw a player in the bar and he kept all their telephone numbers so that, from time to time, he could carry out his own little investigations. On occasion, he'd tell me to get in the sauna with him. There, with us both ostensibly relaxed, he'd start to ask searching questions about my teammates, wanting to know if so-and-so smoked or if so-and-so was drinking too much. I would never grass any one up, but Macari liked to see if I would buckle and spill the beans. I never did.

Lou also got me to run his bets for him, and this is how I finally, unwittingly, became one of his grasses. 'Come here, little Al' he'd hiss at me from some nook or cranny of the ground, before handing me the keys to his Mercedes Benz and a wad of cash. I would drive his Merc to the bookies, shit scared, of course, of getting a scratch on the manager's car. One day he instructed me that I was to drive him to Liverpool to watch a reserve game at Anfield and, naturally, he set about stitching me up.

– 'What do you think of the number four for Derby County?' he asked me during the match.

– 'He's a good passer of the ball but he's carrying a bit of weight' I replied. And I thought that was the end of the conversation.

We'd picked up Chic Bates, the Swindon Town first team coach on the way up and, on the way back, Macari instructed me to stop at a motorway service station so that we could all get a cup of tea together. Sitting around a café table, Lou mentioned Ross McLaren, the Derby number four in question, and Chic started waxing lyrical about him. Lou, relishing the moment, then pitched in, his brow furrowed as if he was making a very serious tactical point.

– 'Hang on a minute, Chic. That's all very well, but little Al thinks McLaren's fat'.

Finally, Lou had got me. After Swindon signed Ross, Lou had great pleasure in telling him what my assessment of him had been: not a great start with a new team mate. Shortly thereafter Swindon made a successful big-money swoop for McLaren. Lou stitched me up once more with this routine, this time before signing the full back Paul Bodin, whom I'd seen play and had quite innocuously described as lacking a bit of pace.

I made my Football League debut for Swindon Town against Newport County away on 12 September 1986 where I played at right back in a 2-2 draw. Things are different now but, back then, your Football League debut was a big deal. This was a fact impressed on you by the league, your club and by your fellow professionals. To enter the Football League as a professional player was to join some pretty illustrious ranks and to contribute to a one hundred year old tradition. And so, having travelled down to south Wales, Mum and Dad were there, watching from the stands.

The next game was against Fulham and I played another few games for Swindon in Division Three. Lou liked to closely observe the culture of the changing room. After watching me fit in, he felt that his 'Little Al' was being bullied around the changing room a bit and had to prove himself. He encouraged me to open my mouth more, to bite back when I received criticism. So, one day, finding myself the butt of some throwaway half-time comment from Chris Kamara, our super-fit midfield general, I exploded in rage. It just happened to be Kammy, but it could have been anyone. Kamara was taken aback. Lou seemed pleased.

My problem, though, was that I had joined a team of established professionals who were romping up the leagues. That season Swindon would gain their second successive promotion under Lou, up to Division Two. Meanwhile, I was settling in at Swindon, having moved into new digs with husband and wife Harold and Alma Coburn. Harold and Alma were a generous and warm couple who made their house a home from home for me. The Coburns looked after me very well for three years in their home along with Colin Calderwood, Nicky Summerbee, Fraser Digby, Nick Hammond and Neil Tomlinson. Lou, however, thought that 'Little Al' needed to learn how to handle himself. To beef up. To rough it a bit. To perform alongside, as he put it, 'big, hard, hairy-arsed pros'. And so I found myself loaned out to Torquay United for the final sixteen games of the 1986-87 season.

Joining Torquay was a baptism of fire into the frantic world of lower league relegation struggles. The West Country club were managed by ferocious Welshman Stuart Morgan and, with just a few matches left, were staring relegation from the Football League in the face. I endeared myself to the home faithful by scoring at home in the local derby against Exeter City (my first league goal) and netting three times for the club after that. But we headed into the final match of that season on 47 points, needing to get a result against Crewe Alexandra and hoping that Lincoln City, above us by a point, slipped up. Crewe, however, boasted a prolific goalscorer in the shape of my former United team mate David Platt. By half-time Platty had made it 2-0 to Crewe. The home crowd, despairing of the team's efforts, became restless. The police responded by bringing out their dogs to keep order. With just minutes to go until the final whistle we were 2-1 down and staring into the abyss. We won a throw-in deep in Crewe's half and our right back, Jim McNicholl, who had pulled a goal back for us, sprinted up to take it.

What happened next has gone down in footballing folklore in that corner of England. In stooping to pick up the ball, Jim somehow spooked one of the police dogs, who sunk his teeth deep into his leg. Jim screamed in pain as policemen struggled to get the dog to release his leg. As he needed treatment, the referee added time onto the end of the second half. Incredibly, with Jim now bandaged up, manager Stuart Morgan insisted he stay on the pitch to take the long throw. Poor old Jim, ball in hands, limped up to the touchline, and launched the ball towards an impending goalmouth scramble in Crewe's box. The ball seemed to float in the air for an age before being flicked on by a Crewe defender and finding its way to Paul Dobson, whose weak shot hit the post before trickling over the line. Cue ecstatic celebrations from players and fans. That goal sent Lincoln City down to the Conference on goal difference and kept Torquay up. In keeping with the crazy logic of 'luck' in football, the police dog came to be regarded as a charm by the fans. The

Chairman agreed and gave the Alsatian in question a free season ticket for life and steak for dinner every day for a year. When the dog died, the club had him stuffed and mounted in the boardroom.

My loan spell over, I made my way back from the wild and weird celebrations at Torquay to the County Ground. Swindon, having steamrollered opposition all season, were about to contest the play-off final against Crystal Palace to decide promotion to Division Two. But when I arrived at Swindon I found that the bus had left without me! I heard a car horn toot and looked around to see a car full of Swindon Town fans, lads making their way up to Selhurst Park for the match. 'Jump in, Alan' they urged me. So I did. It was hot and cramped in that car, alongside the boozy, scarf-waving lads, but we got there in time to see Swindon defeat a Palace team featuring the formidable attacking duo of Ian Wright and Mark Bright.

Ossie's on his way to Wembley

I had been awarded a two year contract with Swindon for the forthcoming Division Two campaign. It was only an extra twenty-five quid a week, but I was desperate to stay on with the Robins. I knew that it was vital I made an impression so I was frustrated when Lou Macari loaned me out to Torquay again. I played well again, scored a few goals, and Torquay manager Cyril Knowles wanted me to sign for the club. But I wanted to break into Lou's team and so I returned to Swindon a month later determined to keep my place in the team. I did so six games later after Dave Hockaday picked up an injury, when I played against Portsmouth at the County Ground, keeping my place for the rest of the season.

That summer of 1988 I watched on television as Ireland beat

England in the European Championship in Stuttgart. Andy Townsend has spoken to me since about the irony of ruing England's defeat that night before going on to captain Ireland. For me, though, I was one hundred per cent behind Jack Charlton's Irish side. Mum and Dad were cheering for the Republic and so, naturally, was I. It was an emotional occasion: it was Ireland's first match after qualifying for a major tournament and, of course, it was against England. After Ray Houghton's headed goal, the television cameras showed Jack clasping at his comb-over as if in disbelief. But as I watched the Irish team soak up wave after wave of England attack, hit the crossbar, and successfully snuff out the combined threat of Bryan Robson, Peter Beardsley and Gary Lineker, it was evident that Jack was turning a lacklustre footballing nation into a force to be reckoned with. While still idolising the likes of Robson, I revelled in Ireland's victory. For me, celebrating with Mum and Dad, there was no contradiction in that. Little did I know that I would soon be turning out in the green of Ireland myself.

By 1989, Lou Macari had been poached by West Ham, so I found myself under the management of the new manager, the famous former Argentina and Spurs midfielder Ossie Ardiles. Under Ossie, it was all about ball work. Our style immediately changed from long ball to a more cultivated, Latin American passing style. I had built up my strength on the ball with the hard and the hairy-arsed at Torquay, but I could also play a bit, and so the new regime suited me down to the ground. Ossie played me behind our front two men, in an attacking arrow. This allowed me the sort of creative licence I craved and I scored eighteen goals that 1989-90 season. It was an honour to play in what was arguably the greatest Swindon team ever. With me slotting just behind our strikers, Duncan Shearer and Steve White, we were devastating on the break. The team was working so well as a unit that Ossie, amazingly, was able to field the same eleven men for sixteen games running. I was in the form of my life and played in all forty-six of the club's league fixtures. Ossie himself made a few appearances alongside me in midfield that season and imbued me with immense confidence to go on and score goals. More importantly, we played beautiful football and Swindon Town soon found themselves in yet another play-off final. This time at Wembley and this time for promotion into the top tier of English football.

My dream season was capped by meeting my now wife, Deby. I was sitting in the Wheatsheaf pub in Stratton, Swindon enjoying a pint with my teammates Nicky Summerbee and Neil Tomlinson when in walked Debs with a friend of hers. For once, the cliché of love at first sight rang true. 'Wow, she's lovely, I have to speak to her' I told Neil. He almost choked on his pint because, unlike some of the other footballers I've played with, I wasn't known for my skill in chatting up women. Undaunted, I plucked up the courage and made my way over to the pretty girl standing at the jukebox, asked her what tune she was after, and started talking. When she agreed to meet again the following week, I was over the moon. On a Thursday night, me and a handful of other Swindon players – Duncan Shearer, Nicky Summerbee and Ross McLaren – had a drinking club. We didn't want to booze the Friday night before a game and so we'd go out on a Thursday instead. And so, on that particular Thursday, I took Deby along with me to South Marston country club, which is just outside Swindon. Since Lou Macari, who did not tolerate his players drinking, had left the club, our Thursday night excursions were not exactly a secret. Neither, though, is it a good idea for professional footballers to publicise their drinking. Ossie found out soon enough and said he would turn a blind eye as long as we kept it low-key and as long as it didn't affect results. For this reason, I did not tell Deby that I was a footballer. Instead, when she asked me what I did for a living, I blurted out the first thing that came into my head and told her I was a lumberjack. That night we enjoyed our first dance and our first kiss. As I held her in my arms, she was surely aware that my grip was not that of a lumberjack. In any case, she soon clocked the truth. Deby's brother was a Swindon fan and so, for that matter, was her ex-boyfriend, who looked across the terraces and was surprised to see her cheering me on as we played Blackburn in the playoff semi-final a few weeks later. He'd taken the unenthusiastic Deby to a couple of matches when they'd been dating. The unexpected reunion made for an awkward conversation.

A few weeks later and Deby, by that stage my girlfriend, was sitting among the seventy-five thousand fans in the Wembley sunshine as Swindon Town marched onto the turf to play Sunderland in the 1990 play-off final. Swindon dominated what was a very open game. We'd already hit the post and forced their keeper to perform some outstanding saves. Then, on twenty-five minutes, I picked up the ball on the edge of the box, took a few touches and let fly. It was about thirty yards out when I hit it and I knew it wasn't the best shot in the world, but it had so much power and pace I was confident it was heading in. Then, enter Lady Luck. My shot took a slight deflection off Gary Bennett and looped over their keeper's leg... 1-0!

Swindon continued to boss proceedings and the score stayed the same. My goal had earned Swindon promotion. Goodbye 'Little Al', hello Big Time! After the final whistle, I looked up to the Wembley scoreboard and there was my name in lights. Ossie Ardiles came running, almost skipping, on the pitch in his little red tracksuit, his face contorted in glee. From the Wembley pitch I vainly scanned across the fans, looking for Deby, for my parents, for my younger sister Diane. Real Roy of the Rovers stuff. In fact, true to the Roy of the Rovers comics I had read as a kid, I was even sporting something of a mullet at the time.

But after we traipsed up the Wembley steps and edged towards the trophy, heart pounding in anticipation, I suddenly realised that something was wrong. Very wrong. No winners' medals!

As our captain Colin Calderwood lifted the cup, there should have been medals round our necks, but there weren't. As we posed for pictures with the trophy I kept thinking 'where's my winner's medal?' And sure enough, a few weeks later our promotion was wiped from the record books. Swindon Town were relegated to the Third Division due to financial irregularities. So much for Roy of the Rovers.

The most annoying thing was that the Football Association knew all about the financial shenanigans at Swindon before we got to the play-off final. When I was on loan at Torquay the season before, the club had made a strategic gamble, one which they would pay dearly for. Swindon were due to play the mighty Newcastle United in a cup game. The Toon were then boasting Paul Gascoigne and Chris Waddle and tearing up opposition for fun. It was unlikely that Swindon would get a result and so the club decided to cover its losses by placing a twelve grand bet on us losing. The players didn't know anything about it. But after the story was leaked to journalist Harry Harris, the tax man soon did.

Since I was on loan at Torquay, I knew nothing of the bet. None of the players did. We were aware, though, of the club's practice of handing us cash bonuses: £100 here, £100 there for good performances. Every club did it at the time, so we were told, and we thought nothing of it. Shortly after Ossie came to the club, we were in for a rude shock. We were pre-season training in St Austell, in Cornwall, and one evening the squad headed out for a few beers. I remember arriving back to my room at around two in the morning, only for the phone to ring at around four. It was Ossie on the line. He was ringing all the players with the news that we had to be up at 6am, to return to Swindon immediately to face questions by Inland Revenue officials over alleged tax fraud.

Swindon Town chairman Brian Hillier, engulfed in the scandal, had been replaced by new chairman Gary Herbert, who boarded the team bus at Gordano services on the M5. He instructed us not to lie and to tell the Inland Revenue everything. When the coach arrived back at the County Ground it was clear that the tax man had come mob-handed: there were around twenty Inland Revenue officials waiting to question every player. I called Dad and told him what was going on. He advised me to tell the truth but not to let the tax inspector into my home. So when I met my investigating official, and he requested that he travel home with me, I explained that we'd had an early start and instead invited him for breakfast in a café around the corner. He quizzed me at length and I told him that I'd received five or six cash payments in my time at the club.

At this stage, none of us were aware of the dodgy twelve grand bet and thought we were getting done for accepting these cash payments. The Inland Revenue official assured me, though, that I wouldn't be prosecuted and that, so I thought in my ignorance, was the end of the matter.

The investigation continued throughout the season and so, before the final had even kicked off on that warm May afternoon, the suits at Lancaster Gate were poised to throw the book at Swindon Town football club. They should have done so before the team and the fans travelled to Wembley. The big money bet was stupid and it was wrong, that's for sure. But, on the back of that, Swindon were also being made an example of for awarding players cash payments and occasionally fiddling gate receipts. At the time, I'm afraid, most clubs indulged in these slightly dodgy practices. Swindon, however, had been caught with their pants down over the Newcastle bet and now we would be the scapegoat.

Incredibly, the FA themselves took a gamble on us first losing to Blackburn in the two-legged semi-final and then losing to Sunderland in the final. That way, Sunderland would go up to the First Division and we, the playoff losers, would be quietly demoted. There was just one problem with their secret plan: Alan McLoughlin's right foot. I'd scuppered the plan, but my status as Wembley hero would be fleeting. The absence of winners' medal was a clear a signal that the FA had never intended us to get promoted and, in the cruellest way possible, would now deny us our triumph.

The cruellest blow was dealt to the club's supporters. The aftermath in Swindon included a civic reception where the champagne flowed. Outside, crowds gathered to catch a glimpse of their heroes on the balcony above. Thousands of delirious fans then milled around the open top bus, standing atop bus shelters and hanging from trees, big smiles splashed across their faces. And then it was snatched away from them in an instant.

By now I was getting used to the slings and arrows of outrageous fortune, but Swindon's demotion was still dreadful for me. Especially since I had been the goal-scorer at Wembley. By the time I found out, though, I was two thousand miles away. I had been called up to Jack Charlton's Republic of Ireland squad for the World Cup in Italy. As one dream had died another, so it seemed, was just unfolding.

3

Italia '90

AN international call-up is a high point in any professional footballer's career. For some, it comes as belated recognition in the autumn of a long career. Others, like me, are lucky enough to win international caps at a young age. I received mine the evening before the 1990 play-off final. And I almost ballsed it up. I was sitting in the hotel at Wembley, nursing a hernia. I'd picked it up mid-season but had told nobody except Deby about it because I was so determined to play good football, to impress Ossie Ardiles, and to take Swindon to the top flight. By season's end, though, it was really starting to ache and I was applying some ice to it when suddenly Maurice Setters, Jack Charlton's assistant, was on the end of the line, offering me his hearty congratulations that I would be travelling to the World Cup finals with Ireland. I greeted the news by telling him to 'fuck off' before slamming the handset down.

After the rocky road I'd endured in merely earning a professional contract, let alone in establishing myself at Swindon, you'd have thought I'd have borne the news with more grace. To explain, my curt and aggressive reaction tells you a lot about the maddening levels of inane banter that come with being a professional footballer. It was nothing to do with the hernia, you see. Rather, I was sure I was the victim of the latest prank by my teammates at Swindon Town. I knew that the Republic of Ireland squad for the World Cup had already been announced and I knew that I wasn't in it. So I thought the phone call was spurious. Trying my best to stay focused on the occasion, there was no way I was going to be the butt of the changing room jokes heading into such an important game the next day.

Fortunately, Maurice called again. This time, he wasn't in the best of moods.

– 'Now listen to me, son. If you do that again, you'll be watching the World Cup at home, not playing in it. Your flight's on Tuesday morning at ten. The tickets are waiting for you at Heathrow. Good luck with the match tomorrow.'

He waited for me to respond, but I was speechless.

-You've made the Ireland squad. You're one of Jack's final twenty-two. Now deal with it.'

And with that, before I had time to apologise, he slammed the phone down on me. I was humbled, delighted and, most of all, embarrassed. Luckily, I'd met Maurice once before. He'd picked me for the first 'B' international Ireland had played for twenty years, when we faced England at Turner's Cross, Cork, in March 1990, in cold, driving rain. That match came after I'd received the two envelopes through the post-box of my Swindon home: the crumpled brown envelope from the FAI and the pristine, white, three lions-embossed envelope bearing England's invitation. After turning down England in favour of Ireland I had a lot of explaining to do. Mum and Dad were happy I'd chosen Irish green, sure. But many of my friends in Swindon and back in Manchester simply could not understand why I had turned down the ostensibly more attractive option of pulling on the lilywhite of England. For them, it was a bad career choice. For me, it was a question of national identity and was the right choice both professionally and morally.

The Irish team that I'd joined were up against a formidable England side which included much of the Arsenal defence of the Highbury glory years – Tony Adams, Lee Dixon, Nigel

Winterburn – as well as players like Matt Le Tissier and Dalian Atkinson, who was in prolific goal-scoring form. Looking at the England 'B' line-up that day I thought back to the two letters arriving through my door, to choosing Ireland over England, and smiled. Players like me, representing Ireland, had an extra point to prove. And prove it we did. We went out there and hammered them. It ended up 4-1 and I scored the first goal, the equaliser, when my right foot drive beat Dave Beasant at the near post. It was extra special since Mum and Dad and my uncle John were there to witness my first international game. But that was a 'B' international, this would be the real thing. The World Cup. The pinnacle of a footballer's career. It was some step-up: a couple of seasons beforehand I'd been at Torquay United, playing in front of a few hundred people and the occasional hungry police dog. That's why I was so sure that Maurice's phone call was a cruel prank.

Mum and Dad, who were staying with me before the play-off final, were beside themselves with excitement and pride. Like all good parents, they channelled this emotion into over-preparing on my behalf. Since I was in the hotel in Wembley, they packed for me, filling a huge suitcase for their son's big trip and cramming into it enough pairs of pants and socks to last me through a prolonged hostage situation. Little did they, or I, realise that all your clothes, your kit, and yes, even your pants and socks, are provided for free when you make a World Cup squad. So after scoring the winning goal at Wembley against Sunderland, off I hared to Heathrow airport, hauling a massive suitcase around with me, and squinting at the departures boards, anxious not to miss my flight. I was bound for Malta, where the Irish World Cup squad were based. I didn't even get the chance to celebrate the playoff win with a glass of bubbly.

But considering what was about to happen to poor old Swindon, maybe that was just as well.

When I joined up with the Irish team in Malta I was hardly expecting the lads to hail the conquering Wembley hero. But neither was I prepared for the frostiness of the reception from some of the senior players. To say that captain Mick McCarthy gave me the cold shoulder would be an understatement. Coming from the ecstasy of scoring a winning goal at Wembley to the chilliness of that greeting ensured that my emotions, already all over the place, were seriously strained.

And the reason for this muted reception? Ireland manager Jack Charlton's infamous last-gasp omission of Millwall midfielder Gary Waddock from the squad. I would be taking his place.

Like the financial jiggery-pokery at Swindon, this was something I knew absolutely nothing about prior to the drama of Gary Waddock's departure and my arrival. I was greeted at the airport by Jack Kelly, a lovely old man in his seventies who was part of the FAI set-up, and who was to travel with me to the team hotel. During the short drive I chatted to this genial granddad and he helped to put me at ease. But he didn't mention anything about me replacing another player. After the taxi pulled up at the hotel steps, I exited from the left hand door, ready to collect my luggage, enter reception, and meet Jack Charlton and the lads. As I did so, I was vaguely aware of someone stepping in to the taxi on the opposite side for the return trip to the airport. That person, I now know, was Waddock.

At exactly the same moment as I was jumping excitedly out of the left hand passenger door, Gary, crushed, was slumping into his seat on the right hand side. Exit stage right Waddock, enter stage left McLoughlin. That moment, for me, encapsulates the hubris of football. The fickleness. The wildly fluctuating ups and downs for young men enjoying a heady but all-too-brief slice of life. Waddock, like me, was an English-born Irish lad bristling with pride at the chance of playing for the country of his parents' birth. He had battled back from a serious knee injury, had played in the last two warm-up games, and Jack Charlton had initially pencilled him in for the squad – only to change his mind at the eleventh hour, swapping him for me. Top-level football management demands such big, cruel decisions sometimes; but anyone with an ounce of humanity had to feel for poor Gary.

I was later to discover that Jack had told Waddock he wasn't going to the finals shortly before I arrived. The players had been larking around, apparently, and Jack had simply taken a jovial Gary aside and quietly broken the news to him. The mood suddenly, utterly, altered. That must have been a horrible moment for Gary but also for the rest of the players. When you are abroad as a tight-knit group of players, an abrupt exit like that knocks everyone for six. As I later discovered, after dumping him Jack had offered Gary the chance to stay on with the squad, but he instead opted to return home (and I don't blame him). After wishing all the lads well for the tournament, Gary left to get his taxi. Then, fresh from the very same taxi, in strides an upbeat young Alan McLoughlin, skipping up the hotel steps dragging an enormous suitcase, pants and socks bulging out of it. Like an excitable kid on his first package holiday. No wonder the reception was frosty.

Neither Big Jack nor Maurice Setters would talk about Gary's exit when I asked them. I think they were a bit upset too.

Altogether, then, it was an unfriendly welcome. John Aldridge soon made me feel better, though, in his inimitably Scouse way. As we bundled into the team bus for training the next day, I took my seat behind the striker. Aldo, a prolific goal-scorer at Liverpool, had just signed for Real Sociedad and was a big name in the game. So I was surprised to see him turn round and say

– 'Tell me, then, lad, are you a giver or a taker?'

Panic set in. What on earth did he mean? I was totally unfamiliar with Aldo's sense of humour.

– 'Errm ... a giver, I suppose'

– 'Well then you'll do for me, lad!'

And with that Aldo shook my hand and we struck up a conversation. It was the first sign for me of the good spirits in that Ireland World Cup camp. I made my full debut in a friendly soon after, against Malta in Valetta, where I played well, hitting the crossbar. On the back of Swindon's promotion, I was in great form and chomping at the bit. If our captain, Mick McCarthy, was still giving me the silent treatment, the other extreme was the room-mate I had been assigned, the Scottish-born Middlesbrough forward Bernie Slaven. Bernie, a teetotaller, was such a live wire that, at times, I was sure he was secretly intoxicated. An example was his phone calls home which, living in extremely close quarters, I was privy to. Bernie would ring his wife and exchange a few pleasantries before hurrying her into putting the family dogs on. He'd then spend ages conversing with his dogs in that dopey doggy voice that people use when lavishing canines with affection. The dogs would bark back eagerly at the sound of their master's voice. This would continue, ad nauseum, every evening, to the extent that I can still clearly remember the name of those two bloody dogs: Shauna and Cindy. That man spent more time on the phone to his dogs than his wife.

Bernie's lingering, loving phone calls to Shauna and Cindy were an early indication of the madcap spirit in the Ireland squad. The phone calls also gave me the chance to leave the room and to try and ingratiate myself with the rest of the players. Our Maltese hotel had been closed for the whole year and had only reopened due to the Pope's visit to the island, which had taken place shortly before our own. It was in the middle of nowhere, half way up a mountain, and, with Jack's curfews in operation, there was very little to do. Life in that hotel really was boring and players filled their time with playing cards or table tennis. During one card school, John Aldridge gambled too much and ended up losing his shirt. But without the social media of today, we were isolated and life got maddeningly monotonous. Every so often Jack Charlton would produce the board game Trivial Pursuit and persuade his always-reluctant players to join him for a game. If you saw Jack approaching with the Trivial Pursuit box under his arm you had to make an exit sharpish or you'd find yourself struggling to answer obscure questions on literature or science while Jack impatiently demanded an answer. Then, after playing for a while Jack, perpetually restless, would himself lose patience and walk off right in the middle of the game.

One day at the hotel, with the Irish press pack swarming around, our kit man – little Charlie O'Leary – managed to alleviate the boredom by almost causing the death of a journalist. Charlie was often to be seen about the place carrying a bag of footballs over his shoulder or lugging a bag of kit around. He cut a distinctive figure, did Charlie, all five-feet-one-and-a-half of him. The journalists tended to leave him alone, instead buzzing around Jack and us players like flies around a cow pat. When one of the journalists who had been newly assigned to cover the World Cup saw Charlie taking a dip in the pool, he asked him if the water was high. The poor guy had only just arrived and had not met Charlie before. Charlie, pointing to his mid-chest area, replied 'the water's up to there on me'. Having received confirmation that the water was high and, seeing Charlie fighting to keep his head above water, the hack decided that he would join him for a dip, only to crack his head open after diving headfirst into the shallow pool. Hilarity ensued. As it did on another occasion when the players were sunbathing around the pool. Jack Charlton, a World Cup winner with England, had inherited his old England manager Alf Ramsey's extreme dislike for his players sunbathing. Jack would strut around the pool like a drill sergeant, assessing a sunbathing player's ability to take the sun, looking him up and down, carefully examining his skin tone, before either moving on to the next prostrate figure, or barking 'fucking get up, you've had enough!' at the unlucky candidate. The fair skinned Steve Staunton would be allowed very little time in the sun and would always be ordered away from the pool first, sulking and muttering away to himself, to the great amusement of the other lads. Imagine Jack's reaction, then, when later on in the campaign he heard that Brighton striker John Byrne, wearing only a pair of shorts, had defied orders and taken out a pedalo in the mid-day sun.

At the end of the week, the Ireland squad enjoyed a night out in Valetta. The Maltese capital was a welcome change from our isolated hotel. So, understandably, having been cooped up for a week, some of the lads went a bit wild that evening. The Irish fans are a fun-loving set of football supporters and those that we came across that evening were great, buying us drinks and, out of nowhere, producing fiddles and guitars and launching into spontaneous sing-songs. No one accused me, or anyone else, of

Family ties

Limerick, you're a lady: My mother Norah with my uncle Pat in Knockaderry, Limerick.

Generation game: At my mum and dad's wedding, left to right, my aunt Mary, my nan Anne McLoughlin, my dad Pat McLoughlin, my mum Norah McLoughlin (née Moran), my nan Bridget Moran and my uncle Pat Moran.

Oh boy: That's me in 1968.

West wing: With my dad Pat and my sister Diane on holiday in Largan (near Shrule), County Galway.

Good times: With my nan Bridget and Diane in Rathkeel, County Limerick.

The early years

He's making a list... Diane, Santa and me.

Short story: Making my First Holy Communion in 1974.

Sister act: With Diane and some of our trophies (above) and getting some tips from my dad in Didsbury in Manchester in 1978.

School boy: At Saint Mark's in Didsbury, Manchester, aged 12.

ur de Dundalk: Pictured left (with my dad behind me) during St Ambrose Boys ub's trip to Ireland in 1978.

oy zone: Lining up for the Cub outs' team in Mosside in 1977, with dad behind me.

Moving on up: With the Boundary Park juniors team at Manchester United's former ground, Newton Heath, in 1981.

UNITED REVIEW

MANCHESTER UNITED FOOTBALL CLUB

CENTRAL LEAGUE
DIVISION ONE
Sheet No.5

Saturday
28th December
1985

Kick-off 2.00 pm

OFFICIAL 85-86 SEASON PROGRAMME

Sponsored by SHARP ELECTRONICS (UK) LTD

MANCHESTER UNITED (Red Shirts, White Shorts)		MANCHESTER CITY (Blue Shirts, Blue Shorts)
GARY BAILEY	1	DAVID McKELLAR
MIKE DUXBURY	2	ANDREW THACKEREY
TONY GILL	3	ANDREW HINCHCLIFFE
AIDAN MURPHY	4	EARL BARRETT
SIMON RATCLIFFE	5	STEVE REDMOND
MARK HIGGINS (Capt.)	6	PAUL LAKE
MARK DEMPSEY	7	JIM TOLMIE
ALAN McLOUGHLIN	8	(Capt.) SAMMY McILROY
ALAN BRAZIL	9	STEVE KINSEY
NICKY WOOD	10	PAUL MOULDEN
MARTIN RUSSELL	11	GORDON SMITH
MARK TODD	12	DAVID WHITE

Referee: Mr.R.H.Andrews (Warrington)

Linesmen: Mr.R.T.Feeney (Shrewsbury) Red Flag

Mr.D.Rowe (Shrewsbury) Yellow Flag

Up-to-the-minute Ticket & Match Information can be obtained by telephone on (061) 872 0199. This is a 20-line, 24-hour answering service.

Welcome to Manchester: On the Manchester United teamsheet for a Central League game against Manchester City in December 1985.

Red Devil: Wearing the red of United in 1985.

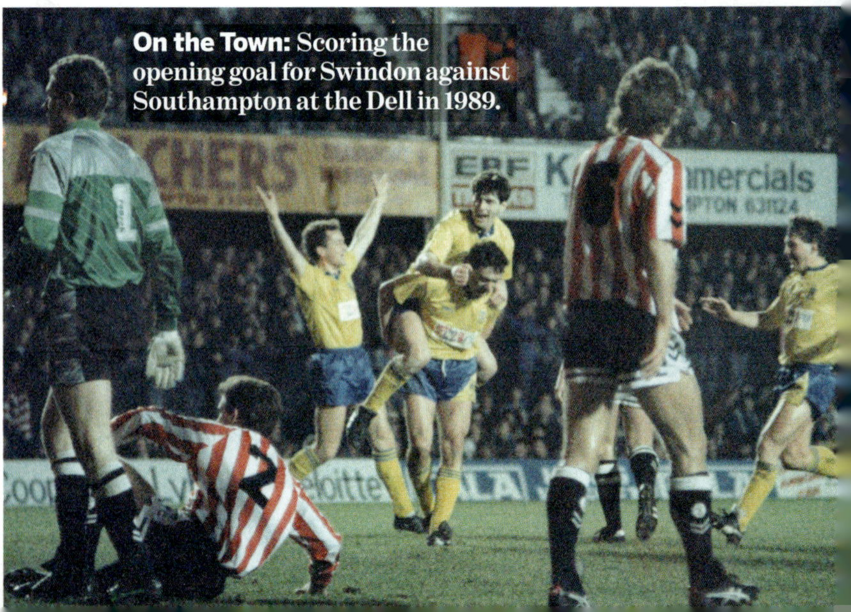

On the Town: Scoring the opening goal for Swindon against Southampton at the Dell in 1989.

Swindon time

Club success: Scoring for Torquay while on loan from Swindon (right); and after receiving the Swindon Evening Advertiser Player of the Year Award in 1989/90.
PICTURE COURTESY DAVE EVANS, 'SWINDON ADVERTISER'

Wembley way

Celebration before the heartache: With my manager Ossie Ardiles and the Swindon squad after 'winning' the 1990 play-off final against Sunderland. However, a few weeks later the club's promotion to the top flight was wiped from the record books and Swindon were relegated due to financial irregularities.

PICTURES COURTESY OF 'THE NEWS', PORTSMOUTH

The joy of the Cup: About to pounce after Nottingham Forest goalkeeper Mark Crossley drops the ball in the 1992 FA Cup quarter-final.

On the edge of glory: Going into battle with Liverpool's Ronnie Whelan in the 1992 FA Cup semi-final.

Get in: Celebrating a 90th-minute equaliser against Blackburn in the 1994 FA Cup third round at Ewood Park. I scored a hat-trick that day in the 3-3 draw.

Unbridled joy: Celebrating a goal for Portsmouth in 1995.

In control: Carrying the fight in my last season as a player at Pompey in 1999.

being a 'plastic paddy'. No one would have dreamt of doing so. It was all for one, and one for all: whether your accent was from Manchester, Mullingar or Motherwell, you were Irish. There truly was an extraordinary bond between Irish players and fans during the Charlton years, a spirit which has dissipated a little over recent years. The Waddock question, however, came up more than once from the fans. Everyone wanted the inside story, which I was unable to provide. I just said I was very sorry for him, which I genuinely was. And with that in mind, I tried hard not to get carried away that evening. Here I was, like the Irish supporters, starry-eyed and sharing a pint with some of my footballing heroes. It would have been all too easy to let the occasion overcome me and get pissed up, which would have worsened already damaged first impressions. Luckily, a good influence was the sober Bernie Slaven, whom I stuck close to.

Perhaps partly as a result of his pedalo stunt, John Byrne never featured in that World Cup campaign. I, however, was delighted when I was named as one of only five substitutes for the first match of the campaign versus England. Here we go again, I thought. If Ireland won, the old questions of the national allegiance of Jack's British-born players would surely be raised by the English media. But if cynical press spin was a sure-fire certainty, so was the commitment of every member of the Irish team to the cause, regardless of birthplace. By this stage, the spirit in the squad was second to none I'd experienced in my playing days. Fittingly, the weather gods were conjuring up a dramatic evening in Sardinia, with a lightning storm raging across a purple-orange sky. A police helicopter hovered cautiously over our heads, and below the storm above. The Italian authorities were evidently expecting crowd trouble and we were bussed to the ground under heavy police escort.

Inside the coach, a tape playing Irish rebel songs, many of which I was familiar with from my youth, was helping us to get pumped up. Melodies of defiance, of grievance, of camaraderie, of determination. A bunch of British-born footballers with misplaced identities celebrating Anglophobia and violence? No. A group of Irish sporting professionals, some born and raised a few miles further east than others, bonding over tunes celebrating the resilience of the underdog.

I had to quickly get over my feelings of excitement and listen to how I fitted in to Big Jack's game plan. 'You are a runnah, son, get forward' was his simple instruction. I had already scored eighteen goals from midfield that season and my job, said Jack, was to press on as much as possible. After an hour of the game had passed that night in Cagliari I stood on the touchline, warmed up and ready to enter the fray, and thought about Deby, my Mum and Dad, and sister Diane watching the drama unfold on telly back home. Of such moments are dreams made. I came on as sub for Aldo and set about following Jack's instructions. Possibly too diligently, in fact. Kevin Sheedy, who belted in our equaliser, recently sent me a photograph of his famous strike past Peter Shilton and there, to the left of the shot, am I: in an offside position! I was ready to pounce, anticipating Shilton parrying the shot into my path. In the event, Kevin hit it so sweetly that the English keeper didn't get a hand to it and, thankfully, neither the television cameras nor the linesman seemed to realise that I was offside.

Aside from Paul Gascoigne, England's real danger-man that evening was Gary Lineker. And sure enough, Lineker scored England's goal on the night, a spawny one at that, but a poacher's finish nonetheless. We also rode our luck a little when Kevin Moran took down Chris Waddle in the box, when

I thought it certain that the referee would award a penalty but instead waved play on. When Jack brought me on, England manager Bobby Robson responded by bringing on Liverpool midfielder Steve McMahon to check my attacking threat and the two of us duelled it out in the Cagliari heat. Then there was Stuart 'Psycho' Pearce, commanding the English back line, who wasted no time in giving me one of his trademark strong challenges by way of welcome. The conditions ensured that Jack's high intensity game left us gasping for breath, but we knew that we had a game plan that worked and we battled away without fear. Ireland fully deserved the 1-1 draw from that game against a very good England side, playing with bravery, organisation and belief.

At the end of the game, I was on a high, especially after swapping shirts with Chris Waddle. Aged 23, it was a landmark to be on the same pitch as Bryan Robson, whose boots I'd been scrubbing as a Manchester United apprentice not long before. Having come through our first match as a World Cup squad, we drank long into the night after that draw with England and I finally allowed myself to unwind, knowing that I'd taken the first steps in justifying my inclusion in the squad to myself to my team mates.

The adrenalin of playing against England that night ensured that I didn't feel the discomfort of a condition I had been keeping secret from Jack and the lads: the double hernia, which I had to have repaired after the World Cup. Perhaps, struggling with the hernia, I shouldn't have put myself through such physical exertion in such humidity. Then again, I was well aware of it before joining the squad. I'd felt it all through the promotion season with Swindon but I'd just played through the pain as I didn't want to miss a single minute of our campaign.

The same went for playing with Ireland. There was no way I was going to tell the Ireland doctor or our physio, Mick Byrne, and deny myself the glory and honour of the World Cup. It didn't affect my appearances at all, but it did cause me grief after games. I felt nothing after the high of the England game but, sure enough, it caused me pain after the match against Egypt, our next group opponents, and I was forced to hide in a toilet cubicle, surreptitiously icing it and take anti-inflammatories.

In that game against Egypt, in Palermo, I again replaced Aldo after an hour. The contest itself was a dire, cagey affair. Mick McCarthy, Jack's trusted lieutenant, was bawling instructions at us, urging us not to take risks, to press, and to keep it tight. McCarthy, a native of Barnsley, could be an intimidating figure and as the tournament progressed there was little let-up in his offhand manner with me following Gary Waddock's exit. During a training match before we played Egypt, I made a mistake which resulted in our 'team' conceding a goal. Mick grabbed me roughly by the arm, hissing 'don't ever do that again!', while glowering down at me from beneath his thick brow. I made sure I followed this advice in the bore draw against the Egyptians, where I again featured in the last half hour.

It was after the Egypt game that the journalist Eamon Dunphy accused Jack Charlton of playing 'ugly football'. Jack responded by storming out of a press conference where Dunphy was present and branding him a 'bitter little man'. I would have to agree with Jack on that one. That spat has certainly had a lot of column inches devoted to it, but at the time us players weren't really aware of it. Back in 1990 there were no mobile phones, no social media. Sure, I saw the whole thing on video a couple of weeks later, but at the time the squad was not affected by it. What Dunphy had chosen to ignore, of course, was the clear fact that the conditions suited the Egyptians better than us. It's tough, very tough, to acclimatise to the sort of heat and humidity we were playing in when it's not in your DNA and thanks to the climate we were puffing about with red faces a lot of the time in Italy. And as for footballing style, Jack's tactics didn't bother me in the slightest. Naturally, I preferred the slick passing and dribbling with Ossie Ardiles, but I was also used to the pressing game of Lou Macari. Ultimately, I trusted Jack. If he had instructed me to hop around the pitch on one leg with my finger up my arse, I'd have done it.

The hotel in Palermo was a different matter, though. While the food wasn't great, it was typical Italian fare: pasta, pasta, pasta and occasionally fish, or soup. The biggest problem was the stifling heat; there was no air conditioning, just those noisy old rotor blade fans whirring round incessantly. What's more, it was three to a room in some cases. Then there was the constant bluster and unpredictability of Big Jack to contend with. One day, in the hotel lobby, I was on the phone to the mortgage company back in England. The World Cup happened to coincide with me moving into a new house with Deby. Prior to my unexpected departure, we'd decided to take things to the next stage in our relationship. Getting a mortgage together was a sign of our commitment to one another. It was as if we were moving rapidly and confidently forward together and, deep in the flushes of love, the thought of our own special place was exhilarating. Deby could leave her parents and move in with me. Little did I know that I would have to iron out the finer details over the phone from Italy after a shock World Cup call-up. So, one day at the Palermo hotel, I was talking money over the phone and probably getting a little exasperated with the whole situation. Jack, coming down the stairs from his room, saw me huddled in the hotel phone booth, deep in conversation about money. I can only think that, to Jack, it must have looked like one of those movie scenes where some desperate character with gambling debts is promising some fearsome gangster on the other end of the line that he'll have the money soon. And I suppose we were in Sicily, home of the Mafia.

Next thing I know, Jack is striding over, taking the receiver from my hand, calmly telling the mortgage broker 'thanks, but no thanks', and placing it down. Jack looked me straight in the eye.

– 'Do you have money worries, son?'

– 'No, Jack, it's ... just a new mortgage ...'

– 'Are you in trouble, son? Come on, be honest.'

– 'No, I was just talking ... it's the mortgage company ... I'm moving house ... you need a certain amount of money ...'

– 'So you're struggling for money, is it?'

– 'No'

Undeterred, Jack promised me a loan of several thousand pounds. And he wouldn't hear another word about it. In the end, I had to insist quite firmly that I didn't need his money. That demonstrates the generosity of Jack Charlton. When it came to money he had another side too, of course, and that was his legendary love of 'cadging' free stuff from people, even cigarettes from the crowd during matches. I came across this first hand when, the day before a qualifier at Lansdowne Road, the squad went shopping in Dublin to relax. I bumped into Jack on Grafton Street. Jack is a big man but he was so laden with carrier bags full of stuff he was struggling a bit.

– 'What are you after, son?'

– 'Err, nothing really, Jack'

– 'Looks like you could do with a new pair of trousers, Alan.'

And with that, Jack marched me into Louis Copeland gentleman's outfitters, pompously announced that he was the famous Jack Charlton and that I was the famous Alan McDonald, and got me a beautifully tailored pair of trousers for free.

Tutti Frutti

After the Egypt match, there were some stirrings from the senior players about the conditions. Frank Stapleton, who seemed to be in one big long sulk from the start of the tournament to the end, joked that the IRA had contemplated blowing up our hotel in Palermo but saw it had already been done. The gag didn't make sense, but I suppose we saw his point. While the FAI's officials were enjoying plush conditions, the players were making do in substandard accommodation. Incredibly, Maurice Setters had actually chosen that hotel after a pre-tournament scout around for suitable places to stay. Frankly, though, I didn't give a toss about the prison-like conditions, I was just pleased to be there. In any case, me and my barmy room-mate Bernie Slaven were creating our own fun to prevent the boredom. All there was in our spartan hotel room were the beds and a fruit bowl. Necessity, so they say, is the mother of invention. So we soon devised a new game whereby I would stand with my back to Bernie, who would launch various different fruits at the bed in front of me from different angles. Seeing an orange or a banana fly past my head, I would have to quickly leap onto the mattress to catch the fruit before it fell. This helped kill the boredom for a while. But for the established players, having to gain permission before seeing their wives or going for a walk was starting to grate. So Jack wisely decided to take some pressure off by allowing families, wives included, to come and visit the players. He also introduced kegs of Guinness to the hotel, trusting us to have a couple of pints to unwind after (and never before) a match.

Our final group game in 1990 was against the Netherlands. I was not named among the substitutes and that was a big disappointment. On the other hand, I knew that Holland were a top team and that Jack needed to play his senior players, even if they were getting a bit precious about the hotels and the food. Ronnie Whelan had returned to fitness and experience was needed. So I accepted the decision to leave me out. The game was reasonably contested but after Quinny equalised for us on seventy minutes, it fizzled out as a contest with neither the Dutch nor the Irish committing to going forward. It didn't make for a great spectacle. I later heard that the referee cautioned Mick McCarthy, along with their captain, telling both men that their teams had to play football. I'm quite sure Mick responded to that request in his customarily brusque manner.

With the match finishing a draw, we finished with identical record to the Dutch. After lots were drawn to determine the standings in the group, Ireland finished second. What an achievement! The football we played wasn't exactly electrifying, but Ireland, in our first ever World Cup campaign, had qualified for the knock-out stages. Like everyone else, I looked forward to finding out who we'd be pitted against in the next round. Thanks to our second place, we heard that we'd be facing Romania. The Netherlands, having finished third, would go on to face West Germany. We dared to dream. This was all breathlessly exciting stuff, but I was also missing Deby an awful lot. Because of my abrupt inclusion in Jack's squad and because Deby was working, she didn't travel over to Italy. Head over heels in love, it was the longest we had spent apart and, as the weeks dragged on, I was spending a fortune on phone calls home to her. We wrote each other long letters, too, about ten each, which we like to look over now whenever we need a giggle.

At this point, it's appropriate to acknowledge an ever-present of the Irish World Cup campaign which certainly helped us through: Tutti Frutti. When players are away from home for long periods together it can often feel something like a monastery. Naturally, young men have sexual desires, but a lot of the time we were under curfew. In those pre-internet days, then, a favourite of the lads was an Italian game show called Tutti Frutti. There was a simple, chauvinistic premise to this show. Two men would compete against one another in a quiz, answering questions from the cheesy game show host. If one got a question wrong his girlfriend, standing beside him, would have to take off an item of clothing. Real smutty, Eurotrash stuff. All bums and boobies, the show was pretty tame by today's standards. But come 9pm in the Ireland team hotel, the place was deserted, with everyone scurrying off to watch Tutti Frutti, usually after a theatrical yawn and with the excuse of 'having an early night'. The lads would be shouting from room to room when the girl's clothes came off, exaggerated howls of delight echoing down the corridors. In high pressure situations, momentary distractions are an absolute necessity and Tutti Frutti soon became the main topic of light conversation to keep us going; we all looked forward to 9pm.

After being drawn against Romania in the next round, we again worried about the heat. The Romanians would be a lot more used to the conditions than we were. They also boasted the great Gheorghe Hagi, who was to sign for Real Madrid after the tournament. On the bus, Mick Byrne tried to dispel the tension by having the tunes blaring extra loud, including our battle song Seán South of Garryowen. Jack was always wary of the British press and he faced accusations of 'treachery' when it was revealed that we would prepare for games by listening to a song supposedly glorifying terrorism. I know the song is about a martyr of the IRA's Border Campaign of the late 1950s, but it is a rousing tune which provided more of a psychological boost than a political statement. All nations have their foundation myths and accompanying ditties and most, regrettably, are violent. It's some leap to suggest that, by playing that song, the Republic of Ireland football team were endorsing the Provisional IRA. It was all part of the mind games. Rumour. Counter-rumour. Propaganda. As a player, I just tried to ignore all distractions and focus on the football.

Regardless, the day of the Romania game, we all felt the nerves. The anxiety was palpable, with Jack doing his usual touchline fretting. We were boosted massively by the crowd, which was predominately Irish, singing 'Olé, Olé, Olé, Olé' throughout, but Romania had an impressive team all the same and we could not break them down either in normal or extra time.

The match, of course, had to be decided by penalties. Up stepped our kick-takers. Sheedy. Houghton. Townsend. Cascarino. All scored, each beating the moustachioed Romanian 'keeper from twelve yards. They were matched by the first four Romanian spot-kicks, which were slotted past Packie Bonner. Then Daniel Timofte of Dynamo Bucharest made the long walk over to the penalty spot and towards the Irish fans behind the goal. Packie, diving to the right, saved his shot, their final penalty. It was now up to our next penalty taker. Up stepped David O'Leary. Everyone on the bench turned to each other and asked the same question: 'Why's Dave taking it?' O'Leary clutched the ball, bounced it, then carefully placed it, and replaced it, on the spot. He then slotted home the best penalty of the evening with the outside of his right boot, sending us through to the quarter finals. Then, delirium. We all made a bee line for Dave, smothering him beneath a massive pile on. I have a bad habit of not tying my shoelaces, so as we all charged over, I hobbled a few paces behind. Dave, gasping for breath, managed to make it out of the huddle just as I arrived, and we shared a hug. I had a lot of respect for Dave for scoring that goal. It takes real balls to take a penalty. I was to score twenty-nine out of the thirty-one penalties I took for Portsmouth, but that was thanks to constant practice. Dave, who wasn't known for his goal-scoring prowess, decisively took and scored that penalty under the enormous pressure of a World Cup knock-out match. It was a brave act, and was followed by the sheer delight it deserved. Packie, crouched on the turf, started crying. Elation.

After the victory against Romania, we pitched up in a better hotel and players were allowed out to see their families. We were also treated to a video showing clips of the reaction back home in Ireland to Packie's penalty save. It was only then that the enormity of it all struck me. We watched footage of people crammed tight in bars, clad in fifty shades of green, in raptures of delight. People from Buncrana to Bandon with their hands raised high, hugging one another, crying, applauding, slapping each other's backs and falling off chairs. Pictures of thousands of happy faces – not just young men but women, children, old people – all delighted, all grinning and laughing and cheering. And all thanks to ten men dressed in green and one in grey. It was truly moving. The entire squad watched those clips together and I think we all had our mouths open. It was my first real appreciation of the significance of that World Cup campaign for Ireland.

In terms of raising the profile of the game in Ireland, that victory over Romania was probably even more significant than the lifting of the ban on Gaelic sportsmen playing soccer in 1971. More than that, though, our success resonated in a rapidly changing Ireland. When we saw the pictures of people wildly celebrating up and down Ireland, and indeed Britain, it was clear that something a bit more profound was afoot. When Jack Charlton was appointed Republic of Ireland manager in 1986 some initially resented an Englishman taking charge. A banner unfurled during Jack's first game in charge of Ireland read 'Go Home Union Jack'. But now people were deliriously happy about the achievements of his team, many of whom, like me, were British-born. In many ways, it was a sign that as Ireland entered a new decade, at long last some of the ancestral tensions were dying down, society was changing and maybe, just maybe, things were starting to look up.

Meeting the Pope

Attitudes towards Catholicism in Ireland were to shift too in that decade, but there was little to indicate that among the country's World Cup squad. After the Romania victory, we were told by Father Liam Boyle, the team's priest, that we were to meet Pope John Paul II. To the vast majority of the players who, like me, had been raised Catholic, the prospect of a papal audience meant a great deal. As a squad, we'd prepared for every game with either an open air or indoor mass performed by Father Liam, after which everyone would feel calmer after collectively reaffirming their faith. Now, through an intermediary, Father Liam had arranged for us to meet the Pope. Charlie O'Leary and Mick Byrne, both devout Catholics, were clearly beside themselves what with the gravity of the occasion, and so had to put up with a good natured ribbing on the bus to the Vatican. But everyone took it seriously. I sat next to Bernie on the coach, both of us inspecting our pristine white tracksuits for any dirty marks.

The audience itself was long and, for a non-Catholic like Jack Charlton, trying. There was lots of kneeling, standing and kneeling. Jack duly fell asleep as the Pope droned on, only to wake up with a jolt. After he'd woken up, I remember seeing Jack signalling to the Pope, which I thought was bizarre. Later, Jack explained this. Seeing the Pope gesticulate to the assembled faithful but thinking the gesture aimed at him personally, he started awkwardly waving back at him. I don't know how Jack managed to sleep because we were sitting very tightly in small wooden chairs and my arse was incredibly sore. Still, it was amazing to be in the serene presence of a man who has since become a saint. Little did I know that we would be ushered onto the stage. I nervously made my way up with the other lads, towards this very holy man. Neither was I expecting him to interact with us. He chatted to Big Jack for a while before turning towards me. I haven't a clue what he said to me, but I instinctively reacted by kissing his ring, after which he touched my arm. There was a very special aura around the man.

Afterwards, we were taken on a tour of the Vatican and got to see the Sistine Chapel. By this stage the whole experience, which was hours long, was starting to wear on the perpetually impatient Jack. When the tour was over he ordered everyone back on the coach immediately. But Bernie Slaven, overwhelmed by it all, decided he needed to buy a memento to mark the occasion. I wasn't sure about this as we were under orders, but I accompanied Bernie to a queue for gifts. To my horror, the queue was about two hundred people deep. 'Come on Bernie',

I said, 'we haven't got time'. 'I don't care what Jack says, Macca, I want to get something'. Big Jack would be fuming, but Bernie felt that he had a special papal dispensation on this occasion. Undeterred, he emerged half an hour later with an expensive-looking gold chain with a big gold cross dangling from it. It looked like something a rapper would wear. We hurried back to the bus, where we were confronted with Jack, apoplectic with rage.

– 'Where the fffffuck have you two been?' Jack could barely get the expletive out, he was that incensed.

Bernie just laughed it off, but I was mortified. Later on I apologised to Jack. By that point he had calmed down. Bernie, on the other hand, didn't appear fazed at all. He had gotten his special souvenir and was smiling like a Cheshire cat. I wouldn't have minded but, days later, Bernie lost the bloody thing. He claimed it was pinched by one of the hotel cleaners, but I think, after all that, he just mislaid it.

Before the quarter final with Italy, in Rome, we all grumbled about having to watch a video replay of the Romania game. By that point, we were all a bit fed up with watching videos of previous games. The accommodation issue had flared up again, too, and this time some FAI officials were forced to move out of their more expensive rooms because they were considerably better than the players'. I wasn't picked for the match and at training in Genoa for the one and only time I found myself a candidate for the infamous yellow jersey: the traditional prize for the worst trainer in the Republic of Ireland team. Ultimately, Mick McCarthy got it instead for being the grumpiest player in the squad.

Yes, it was a World Cup quarter final. But, compared to the clammy fear before the Romania game, there was very little anxiety. At the hotel, players mixed with Irish journalists and the local police, who took to guzzling our Guinness with impressive commitment. I'd like to attribute the pre-match calm to the influence of the Holy Father, but I think the pressure was off simply because all the expectation was on the Italians. Before the game, Jack told us to respect the ref and give a good account of ourselves whatever the result. Not the most inspiring team talk, perhaps, but there was a good reason: the man chosen to referee the quarter final was Silva Valente, who had been nakedly prejudiced against Ireland in a match against Bulgaria two years earlier, as Jack had robustly informed him after he'd blown the final whistle. Jack knew Valente didn't see Ireland as a footballing force and that he would do us no favours, so he instructed the players to keep their cool regardless of the decisions going against us.

Before kick-off, I heard a commotion from the tunnel. As I was standing closest to the door, I pushed it ajar, and a terrific noise made its way into the changing room. It wasn't the crowd singing, it was Luciano Pavarotti, the Italian tenor. There he was, looking like an overweight penguin in his suit, belting out Puccini's Nessun dorma, the anthem of that World Cup. It was weird and wonderful and his voice was very powerful. I was transfixed for a moment before Jack ordered me to close the changing room door.

In the game, predictably, the referee gave us nothing. We lost to a Toto Schillaci goal. And that was that. Jack shook everyone's hand afterwards and told us he was very proud of us all. After shaking hands with Jack I made my way gingerly into the Italian changing room. This time I didn't find Pavarotti, but Sampdoria striker Gianluca Vialli, who was sitting down looking at me as I pushed the door open. I asked him could I have something of his and offered him an Adidas/Opel T-shirt, which looked quite nice in its plastic packaging but which was actually pretty shite. Vialli took off his Diadora jersey and gave it to me in return. I still treasure it. Then we all joined Jack, who was carrying a big Irish tricolour, for a lap around the pitch, to show our appreciation to the fans.

On the plane home, we all enjoyed a few drinks. Mick McCarthy and Frank Stapleton had long abandoned their initial coldness to me and we had all really bonded as a squad. We had surpassed expectations and made Ireland proud. I was pleased that I had two World Cup games under my belt and looked forward to telling both of my grandmothers about meeting the Pope. As we neared Dublin, the pilot announced that he had never seen so many people thronging the streets and would be circling the city several times to show us the crowds. In what was a truly historic moment, there were over half a million people waiting to greet us. Once again, the significance of it all hit me and I felt a lump in my throat as the pilot slowly and meanderingly steered us over the city and then down towards the hot Dublin airport tarmac.

It took us ages to get from the airport into the city and onto an open top bus. The weather was glorious and, basking in the sunshine, throngs of people were lining the streets. I soon overcame my feelings of regret at missing the Swindon street party following the promotion-that-wasn't. This was hundreds of times bigger. The real thing. It felt like half the country had converged on the capital that afternoon. Every adult seemed to have a can of beer in his or her hand, every child a flag. It was time to relax and celebrate our achievements in Italy. I'd enjoyed the adventure and, as a late recruit into the Ireland set-up, was pleased to have played in two of the five games, particularly the draw against the English. We'd gotten as far as the quarter finals and, it seemed, captured the imagination of the Irish people. As the bus trundled down O'Connell Street, one man was far from relaxed. Jack Charlton was his usual frantic self, genuinely worried that little children waving flags would get run over, such were the crowds. Jack is the sort of over-confident character that believes he can turn his hand to just about anything and I half expected him to grab the wheel from the driver and start steering the vehicle himself. But he is also a man of great humanity and, as the bus wound its way towards College Green he started yelling instructions at the bus driver and the Gardaí, warning them that someone was likely to be killed.

Then there was a civic reception on College Green, at the Bank of Ireland building. By this stage, quite pissed up, we were all dying to go to the toilet. The crowd, impatient to see their heroes, jeered the Lord Mayor of Dublin off the platform. Then they were given Big Jack. We listened dutifully as he and Mick addressed the crowds and I gratefully accepted a piece of Waterford Crystal bigger than my head with, as if proof were needed, my face engraved on it. The swelling crowd wouldn't budge. If anything, it seemed to be getting bigger as people made their way down to the Bank of Ireland. Such a public reception was tremendous but, after hours on that College Green stage, it felt marvellous to at last urinate. The gasps of relief coming from the peeing teammates were the precursor to more well-earned pints that evening. That night, as a squad, and to a man, we went out and marked the occasion by getting drunk together in Dublin. It was the spirited climax of a momentous season for me and, after my first taste of the uplifting, addictive abnormality of Jack Charlton's Irish squad, I was hooked.

4

Roy Keane's Rolex

AFTER the high of the World Cup campaign, I had to deal with a nasty hangover: the Swindon situation. I'd scored the goal that should have promoted the club, but thanks to the off-field idiocy, Swinon were denied their place among the elite and, only after a successful appeal against demotion to the Third Division, started the 1990-91 season once again as a Second Division club. Now, Swindon needed money fast and Alan McLoughlin, fresh back from a World Cup campaign and minus the double hernia that he'd been hiding, was their best asset. Manager Ossie Ardiles was very fair and frank about the situation. In late September 1990 he told me that he would be surprised if I was at Swindon for much longer. He knew a big bid was impending and convinced the board to recognise my status by increasing my wages. The club duly doubled my wages and bought me that stereotypical status symbol of the ascending footballer: a big red sports car. I thought I was the dog's bollocks in my new car and, one day in the car park, caught a glimpse of John Trollope – an older man and club legend who holds the British record for the number of league appearances for one side – shaking his head at the young whippersnapper stepping out of the flash Toyota Celica, as he got into his battered old Ford Cortina. He'd seen it all before.

I did not want to leave Swindon. I had settled in the town with Debs, who is a Swindon girl, and had made a lot of friends. But money talks in football, and so I geared myself up for the big move. Ron Atkinson, who had let me go at United, was offering three-quarters of a million to bring me to Sheffield Wednesday, as was Howard Wilkinson at Leeds United. In the end Ossie Ardiles sold me to Southampton for an improved offer of one million. That all but solved Swindon's money problems in one fell swoop. The evening before a match against Ipswich Ossie came to my hotel room to inform me, wishing me well and telling me I needn't turn out the next day. I decided to play, nonetheless, as I owed it to the fans. That was my final game for Swindon and an emotional farewell. As I looked forward to Southampton, I couldn't help thinking about what might have been at Swindon and about my play-off winner that wasn't.

Under Southampton manager Chris Nicholl, a former centre half with the broken nose to prove it, I was told I had been brought in to play behind the front men: Matt Le Tissier, Paul Rideout and a very young Alan Shearer. I would be reprising the role that had worked so well for me at Swindon, and relished the prospect. But the next morning in training Nicholl decided to ditch that idea and stuck me out on the left wing in a conventional 4-4-2 formation. I was now playing out of position and therefore was unable to give my absolute best. I wasn't happy, but told myself that it was just temporary. To my frustration, though, Nicholl insisted on playing me out of position all season long. I played twenty-six games that year and bagged a goal against Manchester City. We finished fourteenth in the top flight, which wasn't bad at all; but then, at the end of the season, Nicholl was sacked. I've since come across Chris Nicholl a few times and he has blanked me nearly every time. I think he partly blames me for him losing his job at Southampton. The last time we crossed paths was, funnily enough, in the urinals at Havant and Waterlooville FC. After he'd finished his piss, Nicholl turned to me and said 'you never did it for me, did you?' before walking out. Yet I had nothing to feel guilty about. Nicholl had spent good money on me to do a particular job and then, without warning, jettisoned the plan. For that reason, Southampton fans never saw what I could do. And that was nobody's fault but Chris Nicholl's. I can't think of another manager who has splashed out a million quid for a player to perform a specific role and then never used him in it.

Nicholl was replaced by Ian Branfoot, a Geordie with a mop of silver hair who was previously manager of Reading. Under Branfoot, I soon found myself in the reserves despite making every single Irish squad under Jack Charlton. The Irish team would experience just as frustrating a time in attempting to qualify for the 1992 European championships at the time. Buoyed by our World Cup exploits, we didn't lose a match in that campaign of 1990/1991. We hammered Turkey 5-0 at home and beat them in Istanbul, which was when the dead cat and the bags of piss started to rain down. So incensed were the Turks at that defeat that an irate fan managed to make it into our changing room after the game. I was taking a pee when he crept up behind me and, trying to remove my tracksuit top, started wrestling with me.

I was caught in an uncomfortable position: simultaneously trying to finish my pee and fend off a marauding Turk from behind. It must have looked quite a sight to Maurice Setters when, hearing the commotion, he came across the tussle seconds later. But he nonetheless swiftly bundled the fan out the door. If it hadn't have been for his quick reaction I could have been knifed (or at least would have ended up inadvertently pissing all over the fan). We drew against England at home and away and I played in the 1-1 draw at Lansdowne Road, during which I passed Steve Staunton through for him to cross to Tony

Cascarino, who headed in our equaliser. Ultimately, though, England qualified above us by just a point. Certain people criticised the style of Irish football under Jack, but in that qualifying campaign we scored double the number of goals England did. And that made Ireland's non-qualification taste all the more bitter.

Back at The Dell, I was expecting a change what with a new managerial regime, but couldn't fathom why I was being consistently ignored. Everything soon became clear when, by chance, I bumped into one of Swindon's club directors while doing a bit of shopping in the town. He asked me how I was getting on at Southampton and I told him about my frustration at making no appearances. By that stage I was not even making the bench. He chortled to himself knowingly. I demanded to know what he was hiding. 'There's a clause in your contract – as soon as you play thirty games, it's triggered and Southampton will owe us three hundred thousand pounds.' The penny dropped. I was being deliberately left out to spare Southampton this expense. The very next day I confronted Branfoot. His broad smile soon turned into a frown and he admitted it. He was holding me back from the team to save the club money. I was furious. Branfoot then tried to play hard ball with Swindon, hammering out a deal with them whereby they would have to accept £150,000 or I wouldn't play for Southampton again, thereby denying Swindon the other £150,000. I was twenty-four, injury free, an international player, and yet I was being used as a pawn. After he had cut this deal, in a league game against Tottenham where I was a substitute, Branfoot put his arm around me and said 'come on Alan, let's let bygone be bygones'. My response to this condescending attitude was short and sharp: 'fuck off, Ian.'

I suppose I simply wasn't Branfoot's type of player. But then neither was my teammate Matt Le Tissier; Branfoot wanted to change the whole ethos of Southampton, bringing in players such as Terry Hurlock, Kerry Dixon and David Speedie. Still, I couldn't believe how Southampton had treated me after splashing so much money on me. Now, my mind was made up. I wanted out. The following week Big Ron Atkinson took me up to Aston Villa on a month's loan. The Villans were doing well at the time and would go on to finish seventh that year. Try as I might, I couldn't break into the first team although I impressed in reserve team matches at Ewood Park and Anfield, playing alongside Dwight Yorke.

Being at Villa Park, it was good to meet up with some of the Irish lads like Ray Houghton, Steve Staunton and Paul McGrath, but the first team kept winning and Ron kept having to explain to me that he wanted to throw me in, but wasn't going to change a winning team. Back in those days, remember, a manager could only name two substitutes. In the third week of my loan I was away on international duty but came back to impress in a Zenith Data Systems Cup game against Coventry where I was thrilled to hear the Villa fans chanting 'sign him up!' Ron responded by sticking me on the bench for the last match of the season against Wimbledon. I was due to go on, but was thwarted when a Villa defender went down injured and Ron had to substitute him for a fellow defensive player. With the summer break on the horizon, I was desperate to get on to Villa's books. After the match Ron Atkinson told me to wait while he spoke to Villa chairman Doug Ellis. When it came to it, Deadly Doug had the option of signing me but instead plumped for two Germans – Breitkreutz and Beinlich – who never amounted to much at the club. Ron explained to me that he wanted to keep me but the Germans were arriving as two for the price of one: they'd be signed up for £400,000, which was my price tag alone. So it was back to waiting again. Back to the boredom and nerves of my teenage limbo, looking at the phone and hoping it would ring. I was desperate to leave Southampton and join the Irish contingent at Villa but it wasn't to be. I found myself back at Southampton the following week. I was pretty miserable.

Playing up with Pompey

Life was not all doom and gloom, though. In the meantime, I'd experienced a very happy moment, marrying Deby on 14 June 1991. As I took my vows I could hardly believe that this beautiful woman, who had caught my eye from across the bar just a couple of years before, was now committing to married life with me. Settling on a wedding venue had not been easy. Deby is Church of England and I am Catholic. We'd moved into a new house together near Swindon and decided to get married in Lydiard Tregoze, which has a beautifully old church decorated with wall paintings and stained glass windows. The church is Anglican, but I agreed that it was our best option. I told Mum and Dad, who would have preferred a Catholic wedding, but who were not bothered as long as it was the right place for us.

We knew that my two grandmothers, on the other hand, would have been upset that it was not a Catholic marriage. As my grandmothers were too old to travel all the way down from Manchester, Mum and Dad arranged for the family to keep it a secret that the church was not a Catholic one. The plot thickened, however, when we went to meet the vicar. To my surprise, it was a woman. For the time, this was quite 'out there' as the Church of England's decision to allow female priests had been taken very recently indeed. I didn't mind, of course, but this tell-tale sign that it was not a Catholic wedding had to be concealed lest either of my two grandmothers noticed, which of course they would have done. Consequently, any photographs featuring the vicar were ruthlessly purged from the wedding photos that made their way back to my two Nans in Manchester.

If anyone is going to turn up late at the church, it's usually the bride's prerogative. But on our wedding day Deby found herself in the uncomfortable position of waiting in the car as the vicar and the congregation anxiously consulted their watches. This wasn't due to a last minute change of heart from me: I was at the church gates with my colleague and best man Nicky Hammond, tapping my watch as well. It was Nicky Summerbee who was the culprit. I had charged my team mate with taking my Mum and Dad to the church. A simple task. Or so you'd have thought. But Nicky managed to get the name of the village wrong and arrived at All Saints church in the village of Lydiard Millicent where, thinking they were early, all three sat and wondered where everyone else was. Two miles away in Saint Mary's, Lydiard Tregoze, we waited for them impatiently. Eventually Nicky realised his mistake and, belatedly, we saw exhaust fumes making their way towards us, heard a car screech up to the church, and saw him and my Mum and Dad clambering out the doors before quickly embracing me and hurrying in.

Debs gave birth to our first child, a girl, Abby, on 8 November 1991. I didn't have much time to savour the moment because just a few hours later I had to leave the hospital for the airport, travelling to Poland for a qualifier. Mick and Angie, the landlord and landlady of the Wheatsheaf – the pub where I'd met Deby – had to drive her and Abby back home in my absence. It hurt to have to leave, and Deby rarely lets me forget it, but I had my duty to do for my country. It was yet another sacrifice I had to make in order to show my loyalty to the Republic of Ireland.

Then, in February 1992, Pompey came knocking. Jim Smith, 'the Bald Eagle', and Portsmouth's manager, was aware of the situation at Southampton and swooped for me, signing me up on a month's loan with a view to a move worth £400,000. Life at Pompey is never, ever dull and the start of my long and eventful association with the club proved this. For a start, the abuse I received from the crowd in my first home game (versus Tranmere Rovers) was something else. I was coming to Pompey after signing for Southampton as their most expensive player ever sixteen months beforehand. The rivalry between the two clubs, separated by just seventeen miles of motorway, is legendary and I was immediately subjected to thousands of people yelling 'Scummer' at me.

The term demands explanation. Portsmouth possesses a proud naval history and is the UK's only island city. Grudges tend to stick and the term 'Scummer' allegedly dates back to a Portsmouth dock strike broken by 'Southampton Company Union Men': scab labourers from up the road. Unusually for a place on the English south coast, Portsmouth is also a resolutely working class city. Arriving in Pompey for the first time I soon got lost in the labyrinthine, cramped red brick terraces that form an urban maze spread across the area. Portsmouth, like Manchester or Belfast, has that red brick proletarian feel. All this is intensified by the fact that, thrown up on a small island but with a population of a quarter of a million, it's also one of the most densely populated cities in Europe. But unlike the red and blue tribes of Manchester, or the green and orange in Belfast, in Portsmouth there's just one tribal allegiance: Pompey. That helps explain the cauldron of noise that is Fratton Park.

Stepping into that as a former Southampton player, you can appreciate how intimidating it was.

At the time, though, I had little idea about the intensity of this rivalry. I started to get an inkling when I was standing in the tunnel before the game and Daryl Powell, a Pompey-born lad or 'Pompey mush' to use the local dialect, turned to me with a knowing look and said 'You must be mad'. 'What do you mean?' I replied. 'Have you any idea what you're letting yourself in for?' Daryl asked. And I have to confess, I didn't. Soon, however, I saw his point. The cacophony of 'Scummer!' that greeted me as I ran out of the tunnel was deafening. I looked over to Daryl, who was sniggering away to himself. When I think back to that baptism of fire at Fratton Park, I can't help but contrast it to the reception I received as part of the Republic of Ireland team in Belfast in November 1993. If anything, I think the abuse I got when joining Portsmouth from Southampton was worse because, as I saw it, it was a footballing hatred rather than an ethnic/sectarian hatred. That might sound strange, but the 'Scummer' taunts were relentless. They persisted, even after I scored a goal and made a goal on my home debut, which we won 4-0. Even after I had turned in several man of the match performances for my new club. Even after I had scored the winner against Nottingham Forest in Pompey's great FA Cup run that year.

That 1992 FA Cup quarter final match against Nottingham Forest was to be my first encounter with a man who would have a seismic impact on football in Ireland and across the water too: Roy Keane. The young Roy was like a bull in a china shop, in the very best sense of the term. He seemed to be all over the pitch, flinging himself into tackles, threading passes, mopping up danger, dribbling forward, contesting every header. I looked at this young Corkonian and immediately realised the massive potential in his dynamism and aggression. With Pompey pressing early-on, Roy's team mate and my old foe from Italia '90, Stuart Pearce, clattered into our own young star, Darren Anderton, leaving him in a heap by the touchline before calmly jogging back to their box. He'd given me a similar welcome in Cagliari. They didn't call him 'Psycho' for nothing and the referee awarded Pompey a free kick. When it came to crosses, Jim Smith had instructed me to stand in front of the unfortunately named Forest goalkeeper, Mark Crossley, as he didn't rate him in the air and, sure enough, when the free kick came in and Crossley duly spilled it, I was there to bundle it in. It wasn't the most sophisticated of finishes; it was what some call a 'Chinese goal' in that it trickled from my knee, off my shin pad and onto my toe: a 'knee-shin-toe' if you will.

After some stout defending for the rest of the match, we held out. My goal had put Pompey through to the FA Cup semi-final. After the final whistle, with Pompey fans streaming onto the pitch to celebrate our win, I received a hard punch to the back of the head. Thinking it was to do with the anti-Scummer hostility, I turned around, angry; I'd scored the winning goal, for God's sake, surely I didn't deserve this just because I'd turned out for the rival club? Pitch invasions can be scary and as a player your first reaction is to head for the changing rooms, but this time I just saw red. I was ready to grab this hooligan by the collar and give him a piece of my mind. But as I turned I discovered that it wasn't a Pompey fan who'd hit me, but a ruddy faced old man wearing a green jumper: Nottingham Forest manager Brian Clough. Now Cloughie had a reputation for striking marauding football fans, but on this occasion, he'd just wanted to get my attention! He put his arm around my shoulder. With the melee on the pitch, he explained, it was the only way he could get me to turn around as he'd been shouting at me but I hadn't heard above the din. Before I could reply, he was off. After explaining himself, he shook my hand, said 'well done, young man, very well played', and skipped off towards the touchline.

In my post-match interview with the BBC's Barry Davies, smartly turned out in check suit and tie, I calmly reflected that the early goal had made for a tense encounter and that we never settled comfortably into the win. I was trying my best to come across as professional and composed since inside I was screaming 'yippee!' and the fans were still romping all over the place behind me. But by the time Pompey's FA Cup semi-final against Liverpool came round, I think I had fallen in love with the Pompey fans and vice versa. I'm a working class lad from Manchester and I felt an affinity with the Pompey faithful that was absent at Southampton. Even the 'Scummer' taunts were starting to die down, if only a little. The Pompey fans and the media were starting to stoke up memories of Portsmouth's famous cup victory of 1939, the last time the club had won the competition and the last cup final played before the Second World War. Thanks to Adolf Hitler, the FA Cup was suspended for the duration of the war and Pompey, as every pub quiz aficionado knows, duly hold the record for retaining the trophy for the greatest number of consecutive years: seven.

As it turned out, Pompey were desperately unlucky not to make the final that year. In the semi-final draw we could have been pitted against Norwich or Sunderland, but we got the titans: Liverpool. The tie was played at Highbury. We matched them in every department and I had two good efforts saved, one cleared off the line by Ray Houghton and one palmed away by Bruce Grobbelaar. It was my job to keep their Irish danger-man

Ronnie Whelan in my pocket and I man-marked him out of the game. This was no mean feat as Ronnie had one of the best touches I've ever seen. The one time he escaped me he landed a nasty challenge on Mark Chamberlain, which Mark still mentions to this day. That was Ronnie, though, for a slight little bloke he could be a nasty bugger. The game, ending in stalemate, drifted into extra time. Then, in the dying embers, it all came alive.

109 minutes: I'm substituted off for Guy Whittingham.

111 minutes: Young Darren Anderton puts us ahead with a calmly taken strike which Bruce Grobbelaar can only get a hand to.

116 minutes: John Barnes floats in a free kick, it hits the post, and Ronnie Whelan – now completely unmarked – knocks in the rebound.

Now, I know that if I had still been on and marking Ronnie, there's no way he would have got to that ball first. But thanks to his equaliser the match ended 1-1 and would be resolved in a midweek replay at Villa Park. Pompey had come within just three minutes of the club's first cup final since Adolf Hitler had marched all over Europe.

In the replay I hit the crossbar when I should have scored. I thought the ball had gone out for a corner kick when it was actually crossed in to my feet. Because I had been shouting at the ref, demanding a corner, I was looking away when I turned to unexpectedly find the ball under my left foot. I instinctively swung at it but I was leaning back ever so slightly when I hit it, just a few yards out. I fairly whacked that ball and, to my horror, it cannoned off the crossbar instead of flying into the net. I didn't need to kick myself, Liverpool's Jan Molby did that for me, ferocious whacking the ball into my crown jewels minutes later. In an effort to recoil I'd given myself cramp and this resulted in me being substituted. As the match again drifted to extra time and – this time – penalties, I watched from the sidelines, devastated, as Pompey player after Pompey player missed their spot kicks. Our Cup dream was over.

That summer brought similar disappointment for England. Ireland's far superior goal difference in the qualifiers was what made it so frustrating to see England qualify for Euro '92 instead of us. Still, I wanted England to do well and watched Graham Taylor's side on the telly as they played out soporific nil-nil draws with Denmark and France in their first two matches. Whereas Ireland, I knew, were a team on the up, England were clearly past their best. Many of the stars of the 1990 World Cup had retired, Gazza was injured, and even Lineker - chasing Bobby Charlton's English scoring record - was struggling. David Platt may have broken England's scoring duck in the final group game against Sweden, but England were justifiably dumped out of the tournament by Tomas Brolin's late goal. I looked at the England squad and saw a bunch of unspectacular journeyman pros managed by Graham Taylor, who was well on his way to becoming a folk devil of the English media. Then I considered the talent that Ireland's more impressive boss, Jack Charlton, had at that time: the redoubtable Packie in goal; the great Paul McGrath; Aldo, Cass and Quinny leading the front line; and, most promising of all, that youthful protégé of the charismatic Cloughie: Roy Keane. Missing that European championship was a squandered opportunity for Irish football, alright.

Going to America

Because Ireland didn't make the European Championship in

1992 we were instead pencilled in to play in a strange little international football tournament taking place in America that same year. Named the 'US Cup', it was a four team round robin featuring Ireland, Italy, Portugal and the USA. For the FAI it might have meant something, but for the Irish players it was something of a joke and the tournament quickly descended into one long piss up from beginning to end. It was on this boozy trip that I was to get to properly know Roy Keane and witness the first flaring-up of the Keane/McCarthy rivalry that would boil over so disastrously in Saipan in the World Cup of 2002.

Before departing for America, we played a friendly against Chile at Lansdowne Road. I received a pass in the middle of the park and, just as I was about to take the ball, was barged out of the way by one of my own players, who then proceeded to go on a dribble up the field. It was the first time that I witnessed the single-mindedness and selfishness of Roy Keane. Barging a fellow player aside was simply not the way you did things in Jack Charlton's Irish side, where our togetherness was our key strength. But then everything about Roy spoke of the exceptionality of huge talent. Even his bloody-minded attitude, which irked me, also impressed me. He was young, athletic, competitive and carried himself as if he had the world at his feet. If his Cork brogue marked him out in a changing room filled with English and Dublin accents, his match-day passion soon ensured he fitted in just fine. On the pitch, that is.

The young Roy liked a drink, like the rest of the squad, almost to a man. We were all completely pissed when we arrived in Washington DC in May 1992. The banter was great on the flight over and when we landed at New York everyone was three sheets to the wind. While changing flights at New York for Washington, we were invited into an executive lounge. More free drinks. Then, in Washington, yet more booze. The trip had started as it would go on – soaked in alcohol – in fact Kevin Sheedy, who was unfit, had secured his place on the tour just so he could enjoy the craic.

Shortly thereafter Ireland's ambassador to America threw a reception for the squad at the Irish Embassy in the US capital, a lavish black-tie affair with mountains of fancy nibbles and gallons of booze. The centrepiece was an enormous prawn island, with thousands of prawns arranged neatly around a huge bowl of Marie Rose sauce. Con Houlihan, Irish sportswriter and a mountain of a man, entered, quite obviously the worse for wear, and took to the prawns with gusto, grabbing an enormous king prawn and drowning it in sauce before shoving it in his gob, bits of sauce and prawn dribbling down his chin as he chomped away. When he got to the crunchy bit his face screwed up and he removed what remained of the prawn from his mouth, eyed it disdainfully, and then threw it back into the prawn island before trundling off to get himself another drink. The players weren't much better behaved, craftily slipping bits of prawn in the ambassador's jacket pockets while making small talk with him, and placing prawns down each other's pants and trousers. I almost vomited the next day when I woke up to several mashed up prawns in my pockets.

We all tucked into the free booze and a few of us had to be carried out of the place that evening and I'm sure the ambassador was glad to see the back of us. Every one of us was pissed on that night and one or two also had a drink on them the night before the game, which wasn't the done thing normally.

In fact, when we played the USA at the RFK stadium, more than one of the team was struggling. There was a bit of fun in the moment as Paul McGrath, who had been charged with marking the Blackburn forward Roy Wegerle on set pieces and, lining up for a corner, turned to me, in a fit of near panic. 'Alan', he whispered, trying not to let anyone hear the question he was asking, 'which one is Roy Wegerle?' I had to grab Paul, who is a big man, and shove him in Wegerle's direction. When the corner came in, Paul met the ball decisively with a thunderous clearance that reached the half-way line. What a great talent.

Our next two matches of the US Cup, against Italy and Portugal, were played in Boston. I didn't play against Italy, a match which we lost, but played the full game against Portugal, which we won 2-0 with Steve Staunton scoring directly from a corner. Boston, being an Irish city, spelt trouble from the off. Again, everyone got pissed up on the flight over. Jack Charlton liked to rub in the fact that he and the FAI officials travelled first class while the players were seated down the back of the plane, and would appear every so often with a glass of champagne in his hand, tinkling it playfully. By the time we arrived at our hotel in Boston, everyone was pretty stocious. Jack gathered us all in the hotel lobby and told us that we'd had a long journey and now needed to get a good night's rest. We nodded in agreement and made our way upstairs. After half an hour, guessing that Jack would have dropped off by then, we all reassembled in the lobby and headed out to find the Cheers bar. We all thought it was great fun to sit, as a team, on the bar stools at Cheers, just like the regulars in the TV series. Except, by that stage, we were all falling off our stools. That night ended very late and very messily.

A friend of Jack's, Frank Gillespie, owned a bar in Boston called The Blackthorn and I estimate that about eighty per cent of our trip was spent in that pub. Frank allowed us to pull our own pints and so, once again, everyone was well oiled on a regular basis.

It was end of the season stuff and totally different than if we were preparing for competitive games. Coming back to our Boston hotel after a few drinks at The Blackthorn, I took the lift and headed up to my room on the fourth floor. The lift stopped on the second floor and in stepped a bar man, carrying six bottles of Budweiser. He took one look at my tracksuit and asked me in a thick Bostonian accent 'are you with the squad?' I told him that I was, yes.

He told me he had never met a group like us to shift beer. The poor lad explained that he had been up and down the lift day and night to keep the party going. "You guys sure know how to party," he said with a sense of understatement in his voice. I told him not to judge us on this experience as we normally had to abstain as professional footballers and were letting our hair down as our season had just ended and we were playing a few friendly ties.

In America, like back home, Jack liked to take his squad on a walk together in the afternoon. As we walked through blocks of Boston streets, I would chat away to Roy Keane. We followed the same route most days and Roy would always linger outside the window of a second hand jeweller's shop. After a couple days of this, I asked Roy what he was looking at. He said 'there's a nice little Rolex there, but it costs $1,200'. I said 'are you buying it then?' Roy told me that he couldn't afford it. We left it that day, but the next day he stopped again, eyeing the same watch. He was at Forest at the time and not yet earning megabucks as he would at United. Feeling sorry for him, I bought him the watch. I was earning more money than him and we agreed that he would pay me back in £200 instalments for the next five Irish trips. That evening, we went out and Roy – against my advice – left his prize possession in his room. We came back to the hotel that evening to find that nearly all the rooms had been robbed and, of course, Roy's brand new Rolex had been pinched. No one had heeded my advice to leave their tellies blaring in the room to avoid theft and so nearly every player's room had been done over except mine. Roy wasn't best pleased at the prospect of still having to repay me for what was now a stolen article, but he did, and later, when he'd made it at Manchester United, we'd laugh about it when Roy would turn up for Ireland duty sporting a watch about ten times as big and worth ten times as much.

I also saw the fierce side of Roy Keane on that trip. On the day we were due to fly home, most of the players had gone on an all-day bender at The Blackthorn. I had gone shopping that day with Terry Phelan so was on time to get the bus to the airport. But Roy and several others were missing. Our flight would be leaving soon so, with a few other players, I did the rounds of the rooms, packing the bags of all the absentee players. Finally, with it looking like we'd miss the flight, Roy and the boys appeared. Jack Charlton was furious, as was captain Mick McCarthy. All I heard was a string of swear words but Charlton, I've since read in Niall Quinn's account, said to Keane 'have you any idea how long we've been waiting?' to which the cocky Keane replied 'well I didn't ask you to wait, did I?' It took real balls to stand up to Jack like that, but Roy then did the same to Mick. Surveying the bedraggled Keane, Mick allegedly asked him 'do you call yourself a professional footballer?' to which Roy replied 'do you call what you have a first touch?'

I didn't hear these exchanges myself because they took place at the top of the coach, but they were clearly the first shots of what would be a long running feud between Keane and McCarthy. They were also extraordinary for the time, because nobody, but nobody, spoke to Jack Charlton or Mick McCarthy like that. As Roy took his seat, alone and with a righteous and slightly mischievous scowl plastered across his face, I couldn't help but draw parallels with my own youthful strop on the bus back from France when I'd told Tony Lacey and Joe Royle where to go. Roy had much less justification, but he had that fire within him, and we had all just got a glimpse of what happened when the embers were stoked. Mick, on the other hand, was indignant. As he sat down in his seat in front of me, stone-cold sober, he was still angrily muttering away to himself.

At the time, though, we all shrugged our shoulders at the McCarthy/Keane bust-up. After all, on the plane home, there was more booze. Throughout the American trip, we'd played golf. Ray Houghton, one of the better golfers in the squad, had developed a habit of yelling out 'shank!' when one of the worse golfers, like me, shanked a shot. On the flight home, pissed up, Ray kept yelling this word from the back of the plane, like a naughty schoolboy with ADHD. Soon, we all joined in. 'Shank!' It was getting louder and louder. 'Shhhhyankk!' Eventually Jack, sitting at the top of the plane, cracked. Unbuckling his seatbelt, he stood up and faced us before charging down the aisle. 'The next one of you idiots to shout that word – just once – won't play for Ireland again. Ever!' he announced. Chastened, there was silence for a few minutes before Ray, bursting with mischief, bellowed the word again along with three or four of the lads. Jack was just settling down in his seat after shouting at us, his arse having barely touched the seat, when the chant rang out once more. Defeated, I think he just rolled his eyes and tried to get some sleep while the craic continued down the back of the plane. When we landed at Dublin airport Niall Quinn, who was due to get married soon, was so pissed he had to be carried off the plane and pushed through security while sitting in a wheelchair.

My first fallout with Jack

Naturally, I'm much more sensitive to health issues these days. Yes, that trip was excessive when it came to drinking and, yes, we all should have been more sensitive to Paul McGrath's problems with alcohol. But Roy Keane was later to brand Jack Charlton's Ireland a 'Carry On shambles' and that's not true. The boozy shenanigans did not eclipse the camaraderie of that squad who, when it came to it, proved they could play and would fight for one another as a team. The US Cup wasn't a complete waste of time – many players who hadn't played got games and Irish fans in America got to see their heroes. On the other hand, it wasn't a major tournament, and that explains some of the silly behaviour. But the Republic of Ireland football team was by far from the only set of footballers to enjoy a night on the piss.

After coming back from the US Cup with Ireland, I travelled to Finland with Portsmouth for a pre-season tournament featuring a local Finnish side, Pompey and the mighty Ajax Amsterdam. Playing against Ajax, we struggled to keep our eyes on the ball. The pitch was next to a massive ski slope and, looking up, you'd see skiers launch into jumps from an enormous height before reappearing in mid-air and landing somewhere to the right of the corner flag. Jim Smith, the Pompey manager, was doing his nut, telling us to keep our eyes off the skiers and on the game and the likes of Marc Overmars, Denis Bergkamp and future Pompey legend, Nwankwo Kanu. The skiers were the least of our worries and our full back Warren Neill was having a torrid time trying to mark Overmars, who was just gliding past him at every opportunity.

After the tournament, there was a drinks reception in a big beer tent. The Portsmouth team, like the Finns, got stuck in to the free booze. After a few beers, two of our players – Bjørn Kristensen and Warren Aspinall – started brawling with each other. As they laid into each other with fists, knocking over a table, the Ajax team – Ronald Koeman, Jari Litmanen and company – shepherded by manager Louis Van Gaal, looked on po-faced and disapprovingly as they sipped on their orange juices. With Aspinall and Kristensen still writhing on the floor, Jim Smith came over to me. 'Look at them boring cunts over there' he announced, pointing his wine glass in the direction of the Dutch team, 'they'll win fuck all, that lot!' Ajax went on to win the UEFA cup that year. That says everything about the football drinking culture of the day and how, as the Ajax team proved, it was starting to change.

The 1992/1993 season at Portsmouth was one of my most enjoyable. We had a slow start, during which we took a couple of thumpings to inferior opposition. Jim Smith was rebuilding following Darren Anderton's transfer to Spurs and it was just a question of things coming right. And when they did, they really did. We put together a strong promotion push that year and fielded a great team. Guy Whittingham, the striker who Portsmouth had bought out of the army, scored an amazing 46 goals. Playing behind him, me and Paul Walsh scored about a dozen apiece. I played well that season because I knew that I had to; I had to score goals and create chances, to cause all the problems for our opponents. We were devastating going forward, picking up some crucial wins, most memorably against Newcastle at St James' Park. With Walshie and Whittingham (soon dubbed 'Corporal Punishment') absolutely rampant, we treated the long-suffering Pompey faithful to some very exciting football. Ultimately, we missed out on automatic promotion to the inaugural Premier League by just one goal. A 3-1 home victory in our final game against Grimsby was not enough and, agonisingly, West Ham were promoted while we had to settle for the play-offs. One goal had kept us away from the bright lights of the Premiership. One poxy goal. Losing to Leicester over those two play-off legs was heart-breaking, particularly as I'd scored our equaliser in the Fratton Park tie. We were the best team in the division that year and, were it not for a defeat to Sunderland late on in the campaign, when we had two men sent off, we'd have sailed into the Premiership.

I didn't feature in Ireland's qualifying campaign for the World Cup until coming off the bench that evening against Northern Ireland in November 1993 and scoring that historic goal. But I still travelled with the squad and, on top of coming through a gruelling promotion push with Portsmouth, the long flights and hotel living that characterises international duty was starting to really wear me out. Still, I wanted to represent my country and would have done so at the drop of a hat, which is exactly what led to my first and most serious fall-out with Jack Charlton.

The campaign was going well. Ireland had beaten Albania, Latvia and Northern Ireland in Dublin and had picked up draws against Denmark (twice) and Spain. Next up was an away trip to Albania. Knowing that conditions in Albania, which was just emerging from a unique and cruel communist dictatorship, would not exactly resemble the Four Seasons, Jack took the wise decision that we would travel with a bare-bones team of just eleven starting players and three substitutes. For the next game against Lithuania, three days later, the whole squad would travel. It was the end of a long season and, if anything, I was relieved. I decided to take a well-earned rest and headed home and then out to play a few rounds of golf. Then, while I was on the green, Deby called. It was Jack on the phone. He wanted me to travel to Dublin to meet up again with the squad and then on to Albania. John Sheridan had suffered an injury and was a doubt for the game so I was to step into the breach.

So I made my apologies to my golf buddies, and headed straight home before catching a flight to Dublin to join up with the squad. Then, in the foyer of our Dublin hotel, Jack turned around to me and told me that it looked like John Sheridan was fit after all and that I could go home for now and return to Dublin again three days later for the Lithuania match. I felt the anger well up inside me. I had dropped everything at the last minute to travel over, only to be told that I wasn't needed after all. It had been a long season. I was wrecked. I was looking forward to some quality family and leisure time at long last, and now I'd made a completely unnecessary trip.

– 'Jack, for fuck's sake!'

– 'Alan, I'm sorry, but John's fit. I'm only bringing the bare bones.'

– 'I don't care. I've come all the way here again. I'm not going home only to come back again in three days!'

Seeing I would not back down, I could sense Jack getting angry.

– 'And who do you think you are, to talk to me like that?'

– 'Jack, I'm here now and I'm going to Albania.'

– 'You can't.'

– 'Why not?'

– 'Because there's no room on the fucking plane.'

– 'Well then, Jack, pull one of those fucking FAI officials off the plane, one of those tossers who likes to sit up the front of the plane with you. Pull one of them off and put me on.'

– 'I can't.'

– 'Yes you can. I'm a player, for fuck's sake. And I'm not going home.'

Jack stormed off but the next day, sure enough, I had a seat on the plane. I had stood my ground and proved a point. I'd given a lot to the Ireland team and wasn't going to be treated in such an offhand manner. I'd always done my duty when called upon, even if it meant travelling hundreds of miles just to warm the bench. I'd left the birth of my daughter Abby so I could travel to play football for Ireland in Poland, for Christ's sake. In fact, looking back on it now, that sharp exit from my firstborn's delivery was above and beyond the call of duty. It was, for Deby, the most memorable in a long line of frequent absences from home when on international duty. Absences which were placing inevitable strain on my marriage and the cohesion of family life. Deby's parents, Nora and Sid, were a great help to her, to us, when it came to childcare, but the burden was undoubtedly falling on her. Our marriage was always strong, but with one partner consistently away from home, any relationship will suffer. Being selected and not making the starting eleven was one thing, but being pulled from pillar to post like that was quite another, and I wasn't having it. Just a few months later, I was to score the goal that catapulted Ireland into a second World Cup campaign and made thousands of Irish people's American dreams come true. Yet if Jack had reacted differently, I could have found myself out of the set-up entirely. I think, though, that he saw my point and had to grudgingly admit to himself that I was right.

When we touched down in Albania I started to wish I had stayed at home after all. As we made our way along the runway, my head almost went through the roof as the plane's tyres bumped over pothole after pothole. Looking out the window, I had never seen such abject poverty. The Albanian dictatorship had banned everything from motor cars to men sporting facial hair. The stench of oppression was only slowly lifting. And, everywhere, concrete bunkers. Thousands of them. On street corners. In town squares. In the middle of housing estates. All thrown up by a paranoid regime anticipating invasion. When we hit downtown Tirana teenagers crowded around the team bus and, to my surprise, I saw that they weren't wearing any shoes. Mick Byrne was upset by all this and started throwing Mars bars to the kids from the Ireland bus. This kind act almost caused a riot as they fought over the chocolate, one boy grabbing a Mars bar only to have another knock it out of his hand, precipitating some pretty vicious fisticuffs.

We each received $25 in travelling expenses. It was nothing more than a token payment to us and, back at the hotel, by way of a tip, Eddie McGoldrick gave his money to one of the maids who was cleaning our room. To our surprise, she broke down in tears, sobbing with gratitude. We didn't realise that a weekly wage in Albania at that time was little more than a dollar. Soon, other maids started crowding round, pleading for money too. I handed out my $25 before we headed to the airport. It was my first encounter with real poverty and it was truly shocking.

Six months later, after we'd beaten Latvia, Lithuania (twice) and lost to Spain, we headed to Belfast on that fateful night in November, 1993. I had travelled to the newly post-communist Baltic countries, which just seemed cold and dark. Conditions in Albania were appalling. Yet just look at the malignity of life in that corner of north-eastern Ireland at that time. People were blown to bits on a regular basis. Every news bulletin from Northern Ireland brought tales of misery and bloodshed.

Playing in front of a venomously partisan crowd, the horrid intensity of Troubles Belfast nearly, very nearly, threw Jack Charlton's Republic of Ireland off the tracks. But thanks to my goal, Ireland would be heading to America once again. Out of the darkness of Europe and into the glorious sunshine of Florida, the Irish were coming.

5

American Dreams

A FEW years ago I picked up the book The Secret World of the Irish Male by the novelist Joseph O'Connor, who is the brother of the singer Sinéad, and came across these lines:

'Somewhere over Newfoundland. The inflight video is showing highlights from the Republic's qualifying match against Northern Ireland. The Alan McLoughlin goal sends an electric shiver of pleasure up everyone's spine, particularly, no doubt, the spine of the manager of the travel agency which organised today's flight, who owes Alan McLoughlin a very great deal indeed. Every time the score is shown again on slow motion, there is another cheer from the passengers. After the fifth time, the hostesses are cheering too.'

O'Connor's book describes the craziness of life as an Irish supporter during that World Cup campaign and those lines sum up the impacts of that famous goal. First of all, the strike against Northern Ireland was a multi-million-dollar one, bringing Ireland to America in more ways than one. I'm not going to sit down with a calculator and spreadsheet and work out the value of my goal in pounds, shillings and pence, but you get the point. The qualifying campaign was long and hard and the entire squad had put in the effort, but ultimately it was my decisive goal that meant that thousands of travel agents, hoteliers, middlemen, airline companies and – of course – publicans would make a pretty penny from the Irish invasion of the United States that summer. Not to mention the FAI, to whom the trip to America was one big cash cow which they would milk until dry, sometimes to the detriment of the players.

More than that, though, my goal meant that tens of thousands of Irish people now had a good reason to travel to the USA, many of them for the first and only time of their lives. Forged by famine and emigration, the Irish diaspora in America welcomed the Irish fans with open arms and for many people the trip provided the chance to reconnect with family members. Some met up with distant cousins on their trip to America, some with more immediate family. I was touched to hear of how many people, thanks to my goal, had travelled over to finally visit brothers or sisters, uncles or aunts who are part of the legions of 'undocumented Irish' in America – those people who, after emigrating, stayed on to work illegally, and consequently have never been able to leave America and return home to Ireland for fear of being refused re-entry to the States.

I experienced one such warm family moment with distant American cousins. Or at least I thought I did. Training in New York before the Italy game, hundreds of Irish fans turned up just to watch Jack put us through our paces. As we jogged around the training pitch, I heard an American voice yelling 'McLoughlin! Hey, McLoughlin!' repeatedly from the crowd. I waved politely in the direction of the voice and carried on with the jog. After training, a tall American man and his family, eight or nine people in total, approached me and introduced themselves as relatives. It was obviously a very moving moment for them and, as is common in Irish families, I knew that several of my antecedents had emigrated to America. On my Mum's side alone, two of my Nan's sisters had left for the States, settling in Connecticut; my Nan's first cousin had tried to get to there but was a victim of the Titanic disaster; and my grandfather's brother had left for America never to be seen or heard of again. Therefore, the man's claim was highly plausible.

So I gave them details of the team hotel and invited them to come by that evening so we could chat about it in greater detail.

That evening I met the big man and his entire brood again. In a snug near the hotel bar, he excitedly produced a black and white photograph of my grandmother and her sister. Except it wasn't my Nan in the picture. As he pointed at the photograph and explained how we were related, I kept looking at the photograph and thinking 'that's not my Nan!' It was painful to break the news to him, made worse by the fact that he just wouldn't accept the fact that we weren't related. As he continued to insist that we were long lost family, I saw looks of disappointment and embarrassment creep over the faces of his family and I felt bad. This man had obviously assembled them all early that morning, nervous with anticipation about meeting his cousin Al, the soccer star from Ireland. Now they all looked tired and a bit dejected, except for Pop, who wouldn't accept the truth and was still trying to convince me. The situation was so awkward that I thought for a moment about pretending that we were related, but I couldn't bring myself to do it and, with the man still adamant that it was my Nan in the picture, I had to set him straight, quite forcefully. In the end, I bought them all a drink and headed back to my room swiftly, allowing myself a little smile as I walked away. Little did I know that when it came to madcap American moments in USA '94, my family-reunion-that-wasn't would be just the tip of a very large iceberg.

Hanging out with Larry Mullen

The World Cup groupings threw up tough opposition in Italy, Mexico and Norway and the run-up to our first and toughest group game (against Italy) wasn't too auspicious. We spent two weeks in Florida preparing for the matches and acclimatising to the heat, but lost both Kevin Moran and Tony Cascarino to injury while doing so. Poor old Jack couldn't win with the media either. After the 1990 World Cup, a few of the now-retired players had gone public about what they saw as Charlton's authoritarian leadership. Jack was asked about this by the press in the run-up to the tournament and he responded that he would treat his players like adults, not monks. The Sun reacted to Jack's statement with the headline 'booze on, lads!' That only confirmed Jack's mistrust of the English press.

But Jack had bigger worries. Before the tournament, there had been a change to the very rules of football that would have a big impact on the Irish game. When football's governing body FIFA published its first ever world rankings in 1993, Ireland were ranked sixth in the world. It signified the astounding progress that Jack had made with the Republic of Ireland, taking the team to heights which had seemed impossible when he'd first taken the job and which, today, seem pretty far off indeed. The intense 'pressing' style was clearly paying dividends. But in 1994, before the World Cup, FIFA changed the rule on pass backs, making it illegal for a goalie to handle a pass played back to him by one of his own players. Jack publicly criticised this. After all, the old style of play had suited the Irish team, allowing us to slow the pace, re-energise and get our shape back. When you look at the build-up to Ireland's goal against England in the 1990 World Cup, the benefit of the pass back is clear. Packie Bonner had time to collect the ball calmly, take a few moments, allow the players to get in the perfect position to 'press' the game, before launching it up-field. Now that was all about to change, as the pace of the game noticeably quickened. Compounded by the American heat, the rule change would prove a serious obstacle to Jack's usual game plan. That much was obvious, even in the pre-tournament heat of Florida.

Then there was our captain Andy Townsend's mystery rash. Andy just broke out with huge red blotches across his face one day. He'd also had his hair dyed blonde in the run-up to the tournament, which immediately deflected the banter away from Tony Cascarino. Cass, who has been dying his hair since he was twenty, was always the butt of jokes because of it; I have walked around many a foreign city on international trips with Cass, trying in vain to decipher the writing on foreign boxes of hair dye as Cass sought out the right shade. Now Andy had joined him in dying his mop and, blonde on top and red in face, he suddenly looked like some sort of vegetable, I'm not sure what type, perhaps a radish. Andy's rash must have been due to the heat, but it had our medical team flummoxed. The doctor said Andy might have gotten the rash from touching a plant and then touching his face. The theory that the lads came up with and repeatedly offered to Andy – that it was a symptom of AIDS – was unlikely, and the rash remained a mystery. Despite having seen plenty of doctors since my cancer appeared in 2012, I am no medical expert. This, however, is my diagnosis: Andy's rash was due to the crap sun lotion that the FAI provided us with. This was ordinary sun lotion rather than the special sports variety. The difference is that when you are sweating as much as we were while training in the Florida heat, ordinary sun lotion is useless, and that stuff could well have caused his skin to blotch. Another theory was that it was mosquito repellent; I'd come out in a similar rash previously after using the mosquito repellent that the FAI provided us with and this probably explains

Andy's big red head, a spectacle which provided the lads with endless amusement.

If the FAI, trying to cut costs, had ordered sun lotion and mosquito repellent from Del Boy, I'm sure that's where they got our plane from too. The plane that took us from Florida to New York for our first game was a right state. To call it a rust-bucket would be to glorify it. Remembering the poverty I'd seen in Tirana, I was sure the FAI had chartered it from Albanian Airways. That was typical, once again, of how the FAI would pursue false economies. The plane was falling to bits and as we rattled around in that glorified baked bean tin I reflected on the meanness of our football association. The tournament was one big money-spinner for them, but the players were forced to experience discomfort so that FAI could save a few greenbacks here and there. Once again, conditions like that aggravated the divide between the suits in business class and the players in steerage: a simple and snobbish division which, accordingly, felt like an impossibly large gulf. When the knock-on effects of having a happy, relaxed bunch of players are considered, such penny-pinching is clearly not worth it.

A welcome distraction from the FAI's persistent tightness was the celebrity presence of Larry Mullen, the drummer from the band U2. Larry travelled with us in the team coach to the Italy game, and was with us before and after every game thereafter. Before the Italy game, he sat beside me on the coach. With his shades, earrings, black leather waistcoat, jeans and black leather boots, Larry looked every inch the rock star. I must admit to being a bit star-struck as we chatted about his motorbikes and cars on the way to the Giants stadium. And then he turned to me and asked 'so, what did it feel like to score that goal?' He wanted me to take him through it all in detail: the build-up, the emotion, the exhilaration, the pride. I couldn't believe I was hearing that question from a rock star used to playing to excited crowds in huge stadiums on a regular basis, but I indulged Larry, and we enjoyed a good chat. Then, as usual, Jack Charlton brought me back down to earth. Striding through the bus, he was yelling 'where's that fucking Alan Mcloughlin? If it wasn't for that prat I'd be sitting on a riverbank somewhere now, fishing rod in one hand, cup of tea in the other ...'

As the coach pulled up to the Giants stadium, we noticed the dozens of beer tents scattered across the enormous car park surrounding the stadium. Tens of thousands of fans congregated around these tents, drinking and singing. Entering the huge stadium for the pre-match walkabout, we looked up to see thousands upon thousands of Irish fans and were greeted with a slow chorus of 'Come on you Boys in Green!' which resonated around the stadium so clearly and passionately that you could almost smell the beer off the fans' breath as they sang it. I knew then that there was going to be one hell of an atmosphere that day. Knowing that the vast, steep stands would provide an intimidating wall of noise, Jack had warned us that the split would be about 60/40 in favour of Italian fans. But, looking up to our fans before the game, we knew that our noise would trump that of the Italians. Everything in the Giants stadium befitted the name: the burly New York cops who provided our escort; the sheer size of the changing rooms built for monstrously big American footballers; and, of course, the volume of the chants coming from the Irish faithful.

In training, we prepared for the match by me, Andy Townsend, John Sheridan and Jason McAteer emulating the famous Italy midfield of Donadoni, the two Baggios, and Albertini. Now, seeing these footballing titans in the flesh, the adrenalin started to kick in. Before kick-off there was some confusion over what colour shirts we were supposed to be wearing – green or white – accompanied by the usual flapping from FIFA officialdom and frayed tempers from our side. I reacted by closing my eyes and trying to freeze time, to almost permanently ingest the atmosphere and the anticipation. I told myself that, whatever the result that afternoon, this was the very reason I played football – this moment – with the noise reaching fever pitch, with stands so steep you could barely see to the top, with the exhilarating feeling that something great was about to happen.

And, of course, something great did happen. After just eleven minutes, Denis Irwin's long ball was nodded into Ray Houghton's path by Franco Baresi and Ray, somehow, produced a fantastic lob to put us one-nil up. As the game progressed, and we protected our lead, Paul McGrath put in one of the best performances I have ever seen on a football pitch, commanding everyone and everything. Before the game we were worried about Paul, who was carrying a very sore shoulder injury; you'd never have guessed it from his performance that day, though. There may have been doubts about his fitness, but Paul simply read the game so superbly that he was a step ahead of anyone else on the pitch. Dino Baggio started to stamp his authority on the game after half time as we struggled to keep possession, but there – waiting to intercept every clever Italian ball, every cross, every threaded pass – was big Paul. There were little luxuries for us substitutes, too, not least the air conditioning in the dug-outs. Naturally, though, I wanted nothing more than to leave the nice cool bench and seriously dehydrate myself by running around in a green jersey, red faced and panting. I had secured my place in the annals of Irish football folklore and delivered us to only our second ever World Cup finals, but here I was bench-warming again. Yet as the match continued, and as we held on to our lead, I accepted and understood Jack's decision. It was simply an honour to be part of that historic occasion; there were better, more experienced players ahead of me. I knew that. I never begrudged anyone a spot in front of me because I knew what talent Ireland had at that time. So, with the blast of the full time whistle, I joined my comrades in soaking up the euphoria of having slain a giant.

After the game, the players were bursting with pride. Jack allowed us the chance to celebrate and off we headed to one of the big tents in the car park to sink some pints with the fans. Later, on the plane, the tins of lager were cracked open as we continued to toast a famous victory. Unfortunately Tommy Coyne, our lone striker that day, was quite clearly in severe discomfort. Tommy had run himself into the ground that day, chasing every ball, closing down every Italian move from deep. After the final whistle, in an attempt to get a urine sample from the severely dehydrated Tommy, FIFA medical officials had instructed him to drink as much water as possible. Still, Tommy couldn't piss. So they gave him more water. Eventually, they gave him so much water that his kidneys became flooded. Tommy was very, very ill by the time we were due to depart and had to lie in the aisle as he was finding it too painful to sit down. As the plane took off and started to gain altitude, he began screaming in agony. He was in so much pain I honestly thought he would die. Later on that evening, we heard that some of our supporters back home actually had died, shot dead in a pub by loyalists while watching the match, their support for the boys in green making them sitting ducks for their callous murderers. It was a sobering point in an otherwise wonderful occasion.

I was in a lot of trouble with Deby, too. Pregnant with our second child – Megan – Debs did not travel to America. Of course she realised the importance of my goal and the significance of the World Cup. And yet I know that there she also felt a natural sense of unfairness .While she was carrying our baby, I was off gallivanting once again. I should have been at home making life as easy as possible for her, doing the odd jobs around the home that were needed before she brought another life to our home, giving her love and support. Instead, a World Cup campaign meant that I was away for a good six weeks. And it wasn't as if the tournament was being played in some backwater. We were in the good ol' US of A, after all. At home and hormonal, Deby was missing me a lot.

She called me late that night, wanting to chat and feel close to me. The problem was, although I was back at the hotel, I had just been invited out for a drink by Larry Mullen. Deby asked me what my plans were and, not wanting to upset or worry her, I told her that I was tired and having a quiet night in. After telling her I loved her and putting the phone down, I scurried out for a few pints with Larry, who'd sent a limousine to collect me and a few of the other lads. But, in a stroke of incredibly bad luck, a British camera crew was at the hotel to cover the aftermath of our famous victory against the Italians and the build up to our next game, against Mexico. As I stepped into Larry's party limousine, a couple of tins of Budweiser in my hand, I was caught on camera. Little did I know that, thanks to the time difference, the footage of me getting into the limousine would be shown on the morning news bulletin back in Britain the very next day. With Deby watching. Gotcha!

Slumped in bed after a great night out with Larry and the lads, I was awoken by the sound of the phone in my room ringing. It must have been about four in the morning. At first, I told myself it was a phone ringing in the next room and closed my eyes. Then, I sat up sharply in bed and groped for the receiver. It was Deby.

– 'Alan'

– 'Oh, hi babe'

– 'How was your evening in, then?'

– 'Oh ... umm ... just ... errmm ... very quiet, really'

And then she gave me both barrels. In fact, that's to understate her response. I deserved it, though.

That wasn't the only time I was caught out by Debs. In 1994, Jack recruited Phil Babb and Jason McAteer into the Irish team, a duo who were part of what the media called the 'Spice Boys': a group of Liverpool players of the mid nineties who earned the nickname because they sported carefully-sculpted hairstyles and a party lifestyle. One evening, while we were holed up at a hotel in Dublin on Ireland duty, Jason and Phil successfully badgered Jack to let them go to a concert that night featuring the Irish boy band Boyzone. After the rest of us players finished laughing at the Spice Boys' gig of choice, we demanded that Jack let us out for a few pints too. He relented and we made our way to a bar off O'Connell Street. I had told Deby that it would be a quiet one that evening, as indeed it was supposed to be. But the change of plan meant that when Deby called the hotel, I was not in my room to answer. She then called hotel reception, asking if they knew where I was. At that very moment, John Aldridge was checking in and got wind of the situation. When he later arrived to join us at the bar, Aldo warned me 'your missus is on the warpath'. So off I sloped off to the nearby Gresham hotel to find a phone to call Deby on.

First I had to contend with the Gresham's doorman, who

wanted an autograph, but who later showed me towards a quiet room where I could call Deby in private. I dialled home and she answered.

– 'Hi babe' I said.

– ' I called your room but there was no answer. Where are you?'

Since it was a quiet setting, I decided to chance it.

– 'I'm calling from my room. I was in the shower; I must have missed your call.'

I thought I'd rescued the situation. Alas, I hadn't.

– 'Oh really. I'll call you back then.'

And with that, before I had a chance to protest, she put down the receiver. She called my room again, to no avail of course, and knew immediately I was out drinking and lying to her. Once again, Deby had called my bluff. On both occasions, the guilt made my hangover the next day all the worse.

Captain Kirk meets John Aldridge

Ireland's next group game, against Mexico, was scheduled for a 1pm kick-off. Worse still, it would take place in the climes of Orlando, Florida. This automatically placed us at a major disadvantage and had Jack Charlton fuming. He was quite right, too. For the Mexicans, playing in that scorching midday heat was not a problem. But for us it was to prove almost unbearable. Just as we would have been better able to handle the cold if the match had been played in Russia, so the Mexicans were just naturally better able to handle the heat. Unable to get the kick-off time put back, Jack, with his legendary hatred for players getting too much of the sun, came up with a novel solution: standing to sing the national anthem, several of our starting eleven would wear baseball caps. I have never, before or since, seen a team line up for the anthems while wearing head gear and it was very funny to watch. I think Jack would have had them play in baseball caps if he could have got away with it.

The Mexicans, who were in command of the game from the off, took the lead after half an hour and scored again just after the hour mark. Remembering how dehydrated Tommy had become in the last game, our backroom staff threw plastic bags of water on to the field to our embattled players, which did little to endear us to the fussy FIFA officials on the touchline. The bags looked like those you get from fairgrounds with goldfish in, and as they puffed around the pitch the lads themselves looked like fish out of water, gasping for air. At 2-0 down it now looked like all our graft against Italy would count for nothing. Jack had to change something. Sure enough, Swanny's long neck turned and he faced the bench. As he did so, the substitutes craned our necks to meet his gaze. Jack was confronted with a dozen pair of eyes, all smiling at him, all begging 'choose me' as he decided who to pick.

When he pointed at John Aldridge, I slid back in my seat. Since going into coaching myself, I think back to that moment and to the dreadful feeling of collective anticipation and disappointment when substitutes realise that a manager is making a decision on the spot. To this day, I ensure that I have the names of possible replacements scribbled on a piece of paper next to players' names so that, if necessary, I can immediately replace a player without having to ponderously cast my gaze along the bench and face a dozen hungry faces. Back in Florida, it was not long, though, before we were all craning our necks again. We couldn't hear the commotion but we could see Aldo waving his arms, shouting, and stamping his feet. He looked like an irate cartoon character, eyes popping out of his head, as he remonstrated with some FIFA official. Somehow, between Charlie O'Leary and Jack Charlton, the FIFA official had been presented with a piece of paper with the wrong number written on it and Aldo was kept waiting on the side-lines for minutes on end. All Aldo wanted to do was get on and score and he and Jack, frustrated by what they thought was petty officialdom, were going ballistic. Now, there's something about Aldo and the Mexicans. In the US Cup in 1992, while playing Mexico, I was clattered by one of their players. It was a really nasty challenge and off the ball, so the referee didn't see it. Neither did I see who had fouled me. Aldo had seen it, though, and he made his way over to me and pointed to the guilty party. He insisted I go after the culprit. Otherwise, he explained, Mexico would have succeeded in intimidating us. I did as I was told and, as I watched the two footed lunge and subsequent booking being replayed on the giant screen in the stadium, I looked over to Aldo. His thumb was raised in satisfaction that I had carried out his orders. The ensuing scuffles between the players after my tackle epitomised our team spirit. In exacting my revenge I had picked up my first international booking, but I had proved a point to my team-mates. In 1994, as I looked over at Aldo, blood vessels bulging in his neck, I thought back to that incident. After he finally made it onto the pitch, he wrought further revenge on the Mexicans by scoring a brilliant header from Jason McAteer's cross, a goal that would prove invaluable to our campaign.

Results meant that we needed a draw in our final match against Norway to see us through to the next round of the World Cup. Denis Irwin and Terry Phelan were both suspended for the Norwegian game after having picked up two yellow cards and Jack, after his touchline eruption against the Mexicans, was ordered to watch the match from the stands as a punishment. The game was played back in the Giants stadium and, this time round, it was an absolute (yet necessary) bore. The scoreless draw sent us through, ensuring that we would meet the Netherlands in the next round.

Players and fans alike celebrated our qualification. In fact, every hotel we stayed at during that World Cup finals was packed to the brim with travelling Irish fans. Looking back on this, it was bonkers. It was great to have the fans around, of course, but everyone was permanently pissed. Every time you dropped down to the hotel lobby for a coffee or a quiet walk, you'd be mobbed by dozens of fans. They'd surround you, hug you, try and convince you to have a drink. Then, as you tried to walk away, the singing would begin – 'Olayyy, Olé, Olé, Olé' – a signal to all the other fans slumped over a settee or chair, or maybe deep in conversation at the bar, to arise and make their way over to join the craic like zombies lumbering shakily towards their prey. A smile would break across your face at this, but you'd be stuck for ages, penned in by this mob of adoring fans.

Ultimately, the players tended to stay in their rooms or in the lounge upstairs in order to avoid the mob. Our upstairs sanctuary had a games room where we could play cards and chat amongst ourselves. What's more, Jack had a keg of Guinness in his room and would randomly invite players in for a pint and a chat with him and Maurice, which was always a pleasure. Walking down the corridor, you'd see the swan's neck craning out of the bedroom door and, when eye contact had been made, a long finger curl into a silent 'come here' motion. Jack's hotel room shebeen brought with it a sense of relaxation and homeliness. If you were called to his room for this honour, you found yourself relaxing as you would while sitting down at the fireside next to a pair of favourite uncles. 'Have you spoken on the phone to Deby today?' Jack might enquire. As you responded, he would take to the tap; pour you your pint; hand it to you; and settle back to listen as he and Maurice lit up a cigar each.

If upstairs had the civilised air of a gentleman's club, downstairs was anything but. To add to the unworldly atmosphere in the bowels of our hotel, there happened to be a Star Trek convention being held in Orlando at the very time we were resident. Lieutenant Uhura, the pretty black woman who used to sit at the bridge and take orders from Captain Kirk, was the keynote speaker. Boozy Irish fans, draped in green, started to befriend Captain Kirk and the Klingons. Soon, they were roaming around the hotel together in packs. I got in the lift one day and looked around me to see Mister Sulu and Scottie standing on either side of me, flanked by a couple of Irish fans who were so pissed they could barely stand up. One evening, returning from a bit of shopping, I cast my eyes over to the hotel bar and there were Ronnie Whelan and John Aldridge, both wearing Spock ears, holding court with a collection of pissed-up Irish fans and Trekkies. It was a madhouse and I began to fear that I'd be beamed up or something if I stayed in that hotel too long.

Despite the craic, the hotel choice was a mistake, that's for sure, and Roy – as captain for the next World Cup campaign – was adamant that this should not happen again. It was in the hotel, the day before the game against the Netherlands, that we received the awful news that Andrés Escobar, the Colombian player who had scored an own goal against the USA a fortnight previously and thus left a lot of Colombian drug barons out of pocket with the bookies, had been shot dead. It was a terrible piece of news that only added to the increasingly surreal atmosphere of the whole experience as we prepared for the Holland game.

It was against the Netherlands that the limitations of Jack's tactics became crystal clear to me for the first time. Marc Overmars crossed for Dennis Bergkamp to slot their first goal past Packie Bonner. And when Wim Jonk's shot from way out slipped through Packie's hands to leave us two down before half-time, the writing was on the wall. In the second half, the Dutch shut the game down and dealt with the heat by calmly passing us off the pitch. As Holland passed tidily around us, we continued to play Jack's favoured 'pressing' game, chasing every ball down, pressuring the ball into the corners, and – when it came down to it – wearing ourselves out.

The truth was that the heat simply didn't suit our usual style but Jack wouldn't adapt to the conditions. He hated square passes, little balls across the middle of the park, or long cross-field passes. From day one, he promised that if he caught anyone playing a square ball across the middle he would haul them off, no matter who it was. And he meant the threat. But, in the heat, all this did was play into Dutch hands. Packie was distraught in the changing room afterwards, blaming his error for our defeat. In keeping with the fickle nature of football, he'd gone from hero to villain in one moment. But the real reason that we were out of the World Cup was that our high tempo game simply wasn't suited to the conditions. For the first time, I started to question the wisdom of Jack's plan.

Some, not least Roy Keane, have since criticised the set-up during that World Cup campaign, citing the diet, the training facilities and the arrogance of the FAI. Some of that holds weight: the state of the plane that took us to New York was a disgrace, as was the sun lotion fiasco. The FAI made megabucks from that World Cup but on occasion treated their assets – us players – as second class citizens. On the other hand, some of Roy's criticisms were composed with a heavy dose of hindsight, not to mention the pen of Eamon Dunphy. Most of the time, Roy was a happy camper during that American trip. He liked a drink and would booze with the rest of us. I remember sharing a drink with him and World Champion boxer Wayne McCullough on Church Street in Orlando. Neither were the training facilities a problem. The Irish strategy on liquid intake was poor and so was the diet at times. But that's by today's standards. Back in 1994, we didn't have sports scientists and nutritionists to take care of these things. The Irish set-up when abroad for a tournament was unique in its abnormality, sure. But I suppose I had been to a World Cup finals before, and Roy hadn't, so I was more used to it by that stage.

While based in America with the Irish team during that World Cup finals, I was supposed to meet a certain someone. That someone was my former boss at Swindon, Lou Macari, who was by then managing Celtic and was planning on travelling to the USA to meet me to discuss a potential move for me. With Portsmouth missing out on promotion to the Premiership in the 1993-94 season, Lou had been given permission to speak with me. So too, unbeknownst to me at the time, had my boyhood hero Bryan Robson. Robbo was managing Middlesbrough and starting to assemble a team featuring the likes of Fabrizio Ravanelli, the 'White Feather', and Juninho. Whereas Middlesbrough's interest did not materialise far enough to make it on to my radar, Lou Macari had clearly signalled his intent and was poised to move. Yet just before the World Cup and only eight months into his tenure at Celtic Park, he was sacked. With Lou's departure went any possibility that I would be heading to Glasgow.

Whatever about Glasgow, I didn't even make it to Dublin for the World Cup after-party. Having made the second round, another homecoming celebration was planned for the Irish team on their return to the Irish capital. On this occasion, however, I missed it. It wasn't just that I felt our exit in the last sixteen didn't really merit that sort of fuss, I wanted to be at home with my family. Deby was pregnant with our second daughter, Megan, and our firstborn, Abby, had developed a rash while I was in America. She had to undergo tests to ensure it was not meningitis, tests which Debs – carrying Megan – couldn't attend. I told Jack that Abby needed her Dad at home and he agreed to let me fly home early. Jack was great with things like that and family came first when it really mattered. Thankfully, Abby was OK. Back home in Swindon, I watched the television clips of Jack and the players emerging from their transatlantic flight home. They looked very much the worse for wear and I saw that, despite their efforts to look smart before landing at Dublin, a few ties had been yanked into impossibly small knots, a few suit pockets had been ripped off and shirt buttons were missing. I'm sure that a few beers were sunk down the back of that plane on that journey home while Jack and the FAI suits sat in first class.

With Abby on my knee, I looked at that rag-arsed group of players and thought of the craic we'd had over the last few weeks. Fitting to the occasionally mad atmosphere in the States, some of the pranks that the players pulled at USA '94 were very funny. While based in Orlando, Andy Townsend and I had taken a trip to the local mall, where we found a joke shop. Jack, who was of the old school, wasn't the most tolerant of his players sporting alternative or extravagant looks. So we bought dozens of pairs of earrings and ear studs and, back at the hotel, clipped them on to the ears of every squad member we could find. When Jack saw us all with our ears pierced, he flipped, ordering us to have them removed immediately. Which we did, unclipping them there and then. Andy also bought a Budweiser can from the joke shop which, at the bottom, contained an electrical charge. If you lifted the can up to take a swig, you'd get an electric shock. Andy and I took this into the bar where we were meeting the rest of the team and where we were fortunate enough to come across a guy, pissed as a fart, who couldn't get served. As he remonstrated drunkenly with the barman, Andy pulled out the Budweiser can and set it down on the bar. 'Here you go, mate' he said. The drunk's eyes lit up and he grabbed the can to lift it to his lips, only to drop it as the electric shock surged through him. The poor man was so out of it that he tried drinking out of the can five or six times before Andy, in stitches of laughter, eventually bought him a proper drink.

Poor old Deby was on the receiving end of the worst prank of the trip, though, which was aimed at me. While stationed in Florida, the squad had taken a trip to Universal Studios to see Thunder Mountain and all the other attractions, including the Jaws ride. Jaws was the first film I'd seen as a kid and so I was quite excited about all this, even as a 27 year old. We were ushered to the front of the queue on every ride, which was great, had our pictures taken with Fred Flintstone, and afterwards all piled into TGI Friday's for something to eat. Stupidly, in TGI's, I left my camera on the table while I went for a pee. I was to regret this because the lads seized the opportunity to stitch me up. A month later, Deby offered to have my snaps from America developed. As she waited at the counter, she noticed the girl behind the desk giving her a funny look. 'Would you like to see your photos, madam?' she asked Debs when they were ready. 'OK' said Debs, before turning scarlet, denying that she had taken the photos, and quickly exiting the shop.

Sitting at home watching TV, I heard Deby come in and I was surprised when I greeted her only for her not to respond. She just stomped in and placed the photos on the table in front of me, placing them down one by one. I was confronted by penis after penis. The worst thing was that, after spending so much time with the squad, I could more or less identify which member belonged to which squad member. Some, like Terry Phelan's, were obviously easier to spot than others. I never brought my camera on international duty again.

6

Hard Times

Swanny's Swansong

February, 1995. Ireland versus England at Lansdowne Road. An international friendly in the wake of our World Cup campaign and in the middle of our battle to qualify for Euro '96 – the forthcoming European Championships to be held in England. It was a crisp, cold Dublin evening; the stars were lighting up the clear dark sky, and I was looking forward to the match. This would be the fourth time that I'd faced England while turning out for the Republic. This fixture always seemed to have a little more bite, a bit more fizz and tension than other international friendlies. For me, of course, it was extra-special. All the players knew one another from playing in England. And although England were supposedly technically superior, at that time we seemed to have the stranglehold over them. It was us who had graced the world stage the previous summer, while England had failed to qualify, and that gave us some extra confidence. Moreover, we'd already eased to victory in our first three European qualifying games, beating Latvia, Liechtenstein and Northern Ireland.

The atmosphere in the tunnel that evening was one of competitive rivalry, not hostility. Ireland were doing well in the European qualifiers and England, as the next host country of the tournament, didn't need to worry about qualifying. But as we walked out that night, one thing struck me as strange right away. I looked over my right shoulder and up to the stand behind the dugouts. There were the green ranks of Irish fans. Then I looked up to the highest tier. There, to my surprise, were the

Union flags and Saint George's crosses ... the England fans. This immediately struck me as bizarre. Why had the English fans been plonked up there? They seemed almost to be teetering on a precipice, arms aloft, piling forward as excited crowds do, squeezed against a single safety rail and within spitting distance of the Irish fans below. The booing and whistling during the anthems, which followed, was no surprise. 'God Save the Queen' was drowned out by jeers. 'The Soldier's Song' was met with anti-IRA chants. That was normal, though, and was nothing compared to that night in Windsor Park, 1993.

We took the lead after half an hour. David Kelly scored a great goal from the left hand side after a lovely passing move starting deep from Steve Staunton. 'You'll never beat the Irish!' rang around Lansdowne. And then it started. I was warming up, stretching on the touchline, when a 'missile' – an apple, in fact – stung the tip of my nose as it hurtled towards my head, before coming to rest in the turf at the edge of the pitch. For a second I looked at that apple, nestling in the soft turf, and thought how much it looked like a golf ball settled in the sand of a bunker. For a moment, strangely, in my mind I was back at the golf links, thinking about how I would play the shot out of the sand. Then, reality kicked in. I looked up to where it had come from and saw fists flying, the unmistakable surge and jostle of crowd disturbance, and – everywhere now – big bits of plastic and wood raining down on the Irish fans. Some of those poor fans were now trying to clamber over the advertising hoardings, desperate to get away from the volleys coming from the English supporters above.

The referee blew his whistle and led the players back to the changing rooms via the centre of the pitch, thus avoiding the touchline where it was kicking off. The Irish players were actually in quite a buoyant mood. We were one-nil up and it was all to play for. Like me, every player in those days had witnessed crowd disturbance of one sort or another. We assumed that all the nonsense would die down in five minutes or so and we'd be back out there. But five minutes became ten. Then ten became fifteen. By that stage it was obvious that the match would be abandoned. Jack Charlton, meanwhile, was outside trying to calm things down. As a World Cup winner with England he thought that he would hold some sway over events. But in appealing to the English supporters he was just met with chants of 'Judas'. He looked forlorn, cap drawn low over his face, as he re-entered the changing room.

When I saw the pictures on television afterwards I was outraged, like everyone else. It was reported that the English fans had been infiltrated by the neo-Nazi group 'Combat 18'. On the night, though, I didn't notice the Nazi salutes being thrust about and the 'Sieg Heils' being yelled: it was all part of the background noise behind me. One image really saddened me. The news clips kept featuring a wide eyed young boy, in his Ireland jersey, the picture of innocence and disbelief, seemingly turning to his daddy to ask him what was going on, as if the fun and beauty of football had been forever robbed from him in that instant. I shared that feeling of having been mugged. We were 1-0 up and had effectively had the game stolen from us by a small group of fascist thugs. The whole episode left me incredulous as to the decision to house those English fans in the top of the stand. The Gardaí were well aware of the far right element travelling to Dublin for the match. So why on earth had they herded the very same hooligans on high ground?

Some time after Combat 18 had announced themselves at Lansdowne Road that evening, they were mannerly enough to take the trouble of writing to me personally. Two envelopes arrived at Fratton Park one morning, one addressed to me and the other to Pompey's Jamaican international Paul Hall. I thought mine was fan mail at first but, unfurling the letter inside, it was soon clear that it was anything but. Both Paul and I were English-born but playing for foreign countries, the letter proclaimed. Signed simply 'Combat 18', it warned me to expect trouble on account of my 'treachery'. The club reported the letters to the police, who took the threat seriously. I wasn't frightened about the threat to my personal safety but the implied threat to my family certainly did perturb me. Soon, two special branch men were at my house, instructing me carefully on how to check my vehicle for a car bomb: a solemn ritual I performed diligently every morning for a few months before deciding that I couldn't live my life in fear of Combat 18 and their bigoted threats. Were they even aware of my parents' nationality, or did they think I had qualified to play for Ireland via the 'granny rule' and was thus more of a 'traitor' to England? Whatever the case, I couldn't allow their reductive logic of national identity to scare me.

Looking back, that abortive match against England was a signal of the disappointing qualifying campaign for the European Championship to come. It was as if something in Irish football, almost imperceptibly, had deflated. In our next qualifying game, a home fixture against Northern Ireland, we only managed a 1-1 draw. This was followed by a solid 1-0 victory against the Portuguese, but the most humiliating result of Jack Charlton's career as Ireland boss was just around the corner.

Liechtenstein. Tiny Alpine principality of about 25,000 people. In their last game, our rivals for qualification Austria had trounced Liechtenstein 7-0. We arrived in the capital, Vaduz, and were charmed by its beauty. With the castle overlooking the town, nestled beneath snow-capped mountains, it looked like something from the Disney cartoons about princes and princesses that my daughters, Megan and Abby, watched. The match was played in another picturesque little place north of the capital. I was not included on the substitutes' bench for that game, but I didn't mind too much on that occasion. After all, it was our God-given right to turn up to this place, admire the scenery, and leave with a win. Or so we thought. The Disney fairy-tale soon turned to a nightmare as I found myself sitting through the most excruciating ninety minutes of football of my life. I looked down to the bench below (actually, the stadium was so small that there was no bench for the substitutes, merely a single row of green plastic seats that looked like someone had left them there after a family barbecue) and saw our players cradling their heads in their hands. Ireland threw the kitchen sink at them but nothing would come right. The goal just wouldn't come and, as the match edged towards full time, so came the dreadful feeling that it was going to finish 0-0.

The draw with Liechtenstein was a serious dent to our qualification hopes. And, in the black book of Irish footballing disasters, it must feature prominently. People talk about Ireland's humiliating 5-2 defeat to lowly Cyprus under Steve Staunton in 2006, but for me the Liechtenstein result was far more embarrassing. We had failed to beat a collection of amateurs – butchers, bakers and candlestick-makers, as far as we knew – despite having about forty shots on target. We were to catch an early flight back to Dublin. It was such an early departure that it seemed pointless to go to bed at all, and so the squad took over a bar in Vaduz for the night, drowning our sorrows and – so it seems to me now – drinking a lament for the glory years under Big Jack. Drinking in memory of the good times and in trepidation of the hard times ahead. If I had started to question how long Jack would continue back in the United States in 1994, it now seemed clear that the wheels were coming off. This impression was bolstered when we turned up at the airport only for the President of the Football Association of Ireland, Seán Connolly, to discover that he'd somehow lost his passport amid last night's fun. It encapsulated the low of the Liechtenstein debacle. Somehow, sans documentation, and after much huffing and puffing from the FAI suits, he was allowed to travel.

But the session didn't stop there. Oh, no. We were due to play Austria one week later in what would be a critical qualifier at Lansdowne Road. To prepare for the game, Jack was taking us to Limerick for a week of training and relaxation. For some reason, we were to take the train from Dublin to Limerick. Assembled at Heuston Station and still suffering the after-effects of the Vaduz shenanigans, we learned that the train was delayed by three hours. So we took to a bar opposite the station (Quinny knew the landlord) and continued boozing, to the surprise and delight of a few adoring commuters.

Onto the train. More booze from the trolley. Arrive at Limerick tipsy. Into the hotel. A quick shower and a hearty hotel meal, and then out again. A great night drinking in Limerick City ensued. The next day, we finished training, had a round of golf, and then prepared to head out again. And so on. I remember sitting in one Limerick bar with some of the lads when Jason McAteer, who likes to give the impression of not being the sharpest knife in the drawer, came swaggering in. 'Alright

Love of my life

To have and to hold... Deby and I on our wedding day on 14 June, 1991 (left); and with Deby in Manchester in 2001 (above).

PICTURE COURTESY OF DAVE EVANS, SWINDON ADVERTISER

Daddy cool: With Deby, Abby and Megan in 1996.

Papa: Meeting Pope John Paul II with the Ireland squad in the Vatican City.

Palermo: Wandering the streets of Sicily and training with Ronnie Whelan.

Great moment: With David O'Leary and Paul McGrath after meeting the Pope (above).

Hard to beat: Sharing one of Ireland's greatest ever moments with David O'Leary after the penalty shootout victory over Romania in Genoa.

Ulster Bank
Ireland's SATURDAY Night
Belfast Telegraph
OPEL

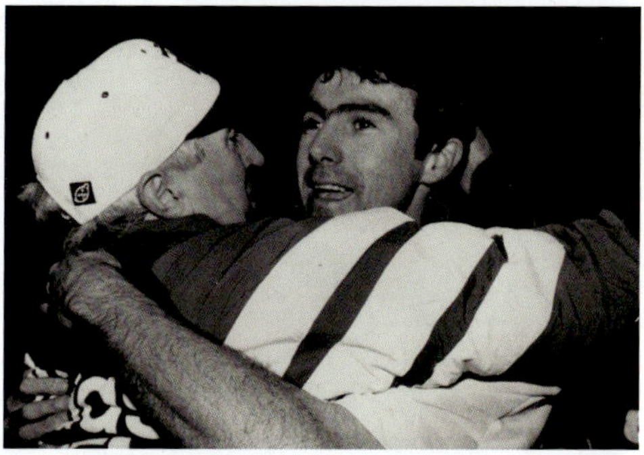

Windsor roar: My equalising goal against Northern Ireland in November 1993, which secured our qualification for USA '94, was my finest moment on the football field.

USA ’94: Behind the scenes

Hanging out: David Kelly, Alan Kelly, Terry Phelan, myself, Roy Keane and An Townsend at Disneyworld, Florida, during the build-up to the 1994 World Cup.

Meal time: Eddie Cochrane, Maurice Setters, John Givens and Jack Charlton tuck in during USA ’94.

Celebration once again: With Terry Phelan, Eddie McGoldrick and David Kelly.

Friends for life: With the legendary physio Mick Byrne and Packie Bonner at Disneyworld in 1994.

American diner: Steve Staunton, John Aldridge and Denis Irwin wait for dinner during the World Cup.

Different shades of green

Here's to you... Meeting President Mary Robinson at Lansdowne Road before a friendly against the USA in April 1992.

Orange crush: Modelling that strange-looking Irish jersey.

Skipper: Captaining the Republic of Ireland's 'B' side to a 2-0 victory over Denmark at Tolka Park in 1992.

Jack and the lads: With Big Jack and a 'Bass Celtic Warriors' team in 1992.

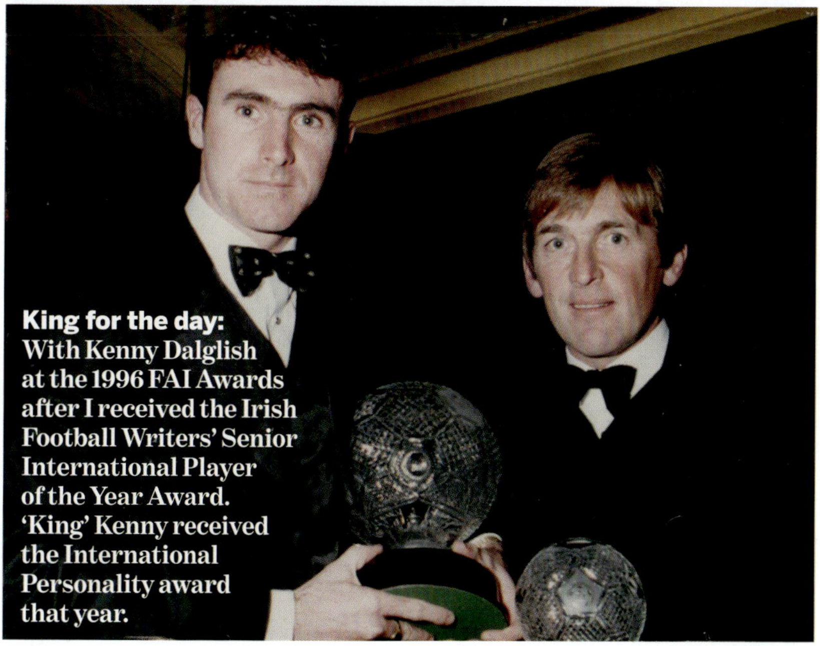

King for the day: With Kenny Dalglish at the 1996 FAI Awards after I received the Irish Football Writers' Senior International Player of the Year Award. 'King' Kenny received the International Personality award that year.

Me and my girls

With Abby, Megan and Deby in 2014.

mate' he addressed the barman in Scouse, 'do you do Guinness here?' We all fell about laughing. 'Come on, Jason!' I shouted at him, since none of us could believe that he was actually asking that question in an Irish pub. The poor barman thought he was taking the mick, but Jason just looked back at him, blank-faced, and repeated the question. I suppose that Jason's then lack of familiarity with Irish culture encapsulates some of the criticism about Ireland fielding English players. But Jason McAteer is far from the norm and is a law unto himself; the stories of his naivety are, at this stage, legion. Jason is a great guy, but I often found myself questioning whether he was really as thick as he sometimes came across. The jury's still out.

The pattern of training-golf-booze repeated itself over the course of the week, or at least the first half of the week. By Wednesday, Jack had cottoned on and declared 'no more going out'. For once, the squad – by this stage the worse for wear after days of heavy drinking – did not respond to this with a chant of 'we love you Jackie, we do' in an attempt to get him to change his mind. By that stage I, for one, was pleased of the opportunity to give my liver some much-needed respite. But Jack's tough stance on the boozing was tainted by his decision to go off mid-week on some little earner, leaving his son John in charge of training. I didn't resent Jack for trying to earn a few quid here and there; after all, all the players did so, particularly when we were in America. A professional footballer's window for squeezing a few extra quid out of his position is ultimately a small one. The player's pool (into which all the extra money earned from endorsements etcetera is put) works on a point basis, with you gaining three points for starting a match, two for coming on as a sub, and one for just making the squad. Since I was invariably earning two points, and sometimes just one,

I recognised Jack's desire to make a few bob on the side. But he should not have left John in charge. Faced with taking orders from someone who hadn't played or managed professionally, we all simply ignored him and did our own thing. After all, the lads had been drinking for four days straight and were in rebellious mood. As John Charlton yelled instructions at us in vain, we completely ignored him, opting instead for a light jog and a five-a-side.

The next day, the Thursday, Jack was back in Limerick. Yet there were more signs that things were just not going smoothly. He insisted on a free kick routine to be used on the Saturday, trying to establish a drill that was just not workable. The routine involved big Niall Quinn performing some sort of blocking role. In practice, it resulted in Quinny getting the ball smashed at him from all angles, with him repeatedly and painfully taking the ball in the groin, the head, the arse and the belly. It was farcical. But Jack, persistent bugger that he is, would not be deterred. On the Friday we took the coach back to Dublin and there occurred one of the more infamous moments of Big Jack's tenure. To my surprise, peering out of the coach window at half past eleven in the morning, I noticed that we were stopping at Harry Ramsden's fish and chip restaurant on the Naas Road. Someone cut a ribbon and Jack, who happened to own shares in that very restaurant, ushered us inside. The challenge, if you wanted to take it, was to push your belly to the limit by devouring a battered haddock so big that it belonged in a fisherman's day dream, along with a mountain of chips and mushy peas. Gary Kelly might have been a little fella, but he put the rest of us to shame by completing the challenge, and with impressively few burps and farts.

That episode has been criticised by a lot of people since as showing the lack of professionalism in Jack's Ireland setup. And they have a point. After Gary Kelly had completed Harry Ramsden's challenge, winning himself a free dessert in the process, the coach made another stop, this time at a local boys' football club for some sort of presentation – all very nice but, like the diet of beer and chips, hardly ideal preparation the day before a crucial game. Viewed in a more sympathetic light, though, Harry Ramsden's challenge was another episode in the good companionship that came with playing for Ireland. The overriding point is this: when turning up for Ireland duty, the norm was itself abnormal. No one moaned about it at the time. What you can't argue with, however, are results; the subsequent back-to-back defeats to Austria really cost us. And if there's one thing of which I'm sure, the week of beer and golf did nothing to improve our performance on that evening in Dublin when the Austrians beat us 3-1.

The run of results meant that to make it to Euro '96 we would have to win a play-off. We were drawn to play our old foes the Netherlands in a match to be played at Anfield in late 1995. The evening before the match was to bring more comedy, this time as we gathered to watch a video of the Dutch team in action. In a private room in our Liverpool hotel everyone sat attentively in rows of chairs, Jack Charlton and Maurice Setters up front, with the players behind them. The Netherlands had a formidable side and so everyone was very serious as the VHS went in the slot and the picture, crackly at first, came on the television. To my surprise, as the camera scanned across the two teams standing for the anthems it showed eleven anonymous faces in orange shirts surrounded by an empty stadium. I squinted at the Dutch team on screen, unable to make out Kluivert, Bergkamp or any of their other stars. After five minutes it became abundantly clear to everyone that this was a video of the Dutch under-21 team. Everyone, that is, apart from Jack and Maurice. The lads started nudging each other, laughter rippling, as we waited for Jack to realise. Another five minutes passed. Still Jack hadn't clocked what was going on. Another few minutes passed. Up Jack leapt, pausing the video. He's finally realised, I thought. But as Jack started lecturing us, I realised I was wrong.

– 'Now, watch Bergkamp'

Jack was pointing at the Dutch under-21 striker, who just happened, like Denis Bergkamp, to have blonde hair.

– 'Now, watch the way he pulls away from his defender. Here.'

Cue hoots of laughter.

– 'What the hell do you lot think you're laughing at, eh? What's so fucking funny?'

Jack's question was met with more howls of delight. Eventually, Andy Townsend told him what had happened. Jack blamed Maurice and gave him a bollocking. Maurice, in turn, blamed the Dutch. Sabotage! Jack's final word on the matter was 'fuck 'em, we'll beat 'em anyway'. It didn't bode well.

The following evening, buoyed by a Liverpool-Irish crowd, Ireland lined up to face the Dutch team. This time, it was the proper Dutch team, as we discovered to our cost. One frustrating memory stands out from that evening. Andy Townsend was substituted for Jason McAteer after 50 minutes. We were already losing 1-0 to a Patrick Kluivert goal and Andy turned to Big Jack and said 'get Al Mac on'. Jack looked over at me slowly before consenting, telling me to start warming up. Adrenalin pumping, I waited for the nod. On seventy-three minutes, Jack pulled off John Aldridge and I got ready to enter the fray. 'I am going to score here', I repeated to myself, 'I am going to score'. I was sure I could be the goal-scoring hero, like in 1993, and salvage our campaign. I finished limbering up and puffed out my chest, ready to run on. Then, to my disgust, I saw Jack telling Alan Kernaghan that he was coming on. Alan was playing well for Manchester City, sure, but he was a defender. To put this in context, we'd started the match with six defenders; the decision meant that seven out of our ten outfield players were now defenders! I confess, I threw a strop there and then. Why, oh why, with us a goal down in a do-or-die match, was Jack taking off a striker and putting on a defensive player? We had to press forward and, like in Belfast in 1993, I felt I was capable of getting a goal in that final twenty minutes. I should have been given the opportunity to the change the match: for the team, and to lift the spirits of the travelling Irish fans. I certainly was more of a threat to score than Alan Kernaghan in my eyes and in our captain's eyes, also. But Jack motioned to Kernaghan and on he went. I am still baffled by that decision. We ended up losing 2-0 and that really was the end of the dream.

Terry Venables comes to Fratton

If Jack had carried on after the failure to make Euro '96 I would have evaluated whether I had a future in international football. The magic of the Charlton years had clearly faded. Jack's pressing game was past its sell-by date and, while I was playing well at Portsmouth, warming the bench for Ireland was becoming increasingly frustrating. Shortly after the defeat at Anfield, Jack was persuaded to call it a day. It was the right decision. I have tremendous respect for Jack and will always be grateful to him for transforming me into an international footballer. He exceeded his brief in making Ireland a force in international football and in raising the profile of the game domestically. The Republic came to be viewed as a powerful force to be respected and feared by opponents. Nonetheless, the time was right. Managerial change was afoot at Pompey, too, where another former England World Cup footballer – Terry Fenwick – had replaced Jim Smith. Fenwick is unfairly remembered as one of the players whom Diego Maradona dribbled past on his way to scoring his wonder goal against England at the 1986 World Cup. But in his playing days, Fenwick turned out as a classy full-back for Crystal Palace and Spurs as well as earning twenty England caps.

Now, it's always tough for a new manager coming in, but I did not see eye to eye with Terry Fenwick on a number of occasions. Perhaps I had become one of those troublesome senior professionals whom I'd looked at with a mixture of awe and dread when I was a young player. Even so, Terry's decisions sometimes left me puzzled. For instance, there was the time he dropped me for playing badly while suffering from chicken pox. I had never suffered chicken pox as a kid and when my daughter Megan caught it, so did I. Despite feeling dreadful, I turned up at a club open day the next morning. Pompey's physio Neil Sillett took one look at me and told me to do a couple of laps of the pitch for the fans before calling it a day. I managed one lap before vomiting. I took the next few days off, sick as a dog, before reporting for duty on the Thursday. At training that day Terry looked at me and told me I looked terrible. Moreover, the club doctor had ordered me not to play that week. Fenwick then asked if I could play on the Saturday! I told him I felt shit, but if no one else was available, I'd do a job for him. In my condition, though, I couldn't promise a world-beating performance. He told me that it was OK, I just needed to play one half. Saturday came around and, lo and behold, he kept me on for the full ninety minutes. I was pale, weak and spotty. The last place on earth I wanted to be was charging around a football pitch. Opposition midfielder Andy Porter kept winding me up during the game, asking me when I had got acne, and if I'd hit puberty yet. Despite my condition I scored a penalty. However, the following Friday, when I was still on the mend, Terry Fenwick pulled me aside at training and told me I had played poorly the week before and that he was dropping me for our next game, which was against West Brom at home. I was seething with anger. As I was when, later on in the season, Terry Fenwick again dropped me, with the explanation that I had not played well in a game the week before. This time I really did have all the justification on my side. I hadn't even played in that game: I was away on international duty with Ireland!

– 'I didn't even play last week!' I complained.

– 'Yes you did' he replied.

– 'No I fucking didn't!' I countered. By this stage I think he realised that he'd made a mistake.

– 'Well, I'm dropping you anyway!' was his final retort.

Terry Fenwick's first season as Pompey manager ended with us in a relegation dog fight. That 1995-96 season was also the one and only time I played against Southampton for Pompey. We lost 3-0 at The Dell in the FA Cup. With all the fierceness of that rare rivalry, and having at last overcome the dreaded 'Scummer' taunts to secure my place in Pompey fans' hearts, the defeat really hurt. In fact, it still hurts to this day. The following pre-season, I was to clash with the manager again. Pompey had bought me for £400,000 but there was a clause in my contract whereby, if I was sold on for more than that sum, I would receive ten per cent of the difference. Terry Fenwick knew this and so endeavoured to offload me to Port Vale for

£400,000 exactly. We were at our team hotel in Dunblane, Scotland, when he broke the news. He told me that it was pretty much a done deal and that Port Vale manager John Rudge was flying up to Scotland to meet with me. I told him that I wasn't going anywhere, but especially not Port Vale, and especially not at that price. Once again, relations between us soured.

With Terry Fenwick floundering, the club badly needed a boost. Enter Terry Venables. Fresh from taking England to the semi- finals of Euro '96, Venables was now unexpectedly bringing his sparkle to Fratton Park as Director of Football. The prospect of his joining the Pompey set-up gave all of us players a lift. Again, it had been frustrating to watch that summer's European Championships on telly instead of playing in it. It was the first major tournament on English soil since the World Cup in 1966 and to miss out was terrible. You couldn't begrudge the achievements of Terry Venables' England, though. Paul Gascoigne's issues with booze were well known. So when Gazza celebrated his brilliant goal against Scotland by lying behind the goal and having water squeezed down his throat, in imitation of the 'Dentist's Chair' drinking game which took place during a pre-tournament trip to Hong Kong, I allowed myself a smile. Gazza's addiction, like Paul McGrath's and a lot of other people's, is very, very sad. But, you had to hand it to him: as a reply to an English press pack whose relentless pursuit of him was fuelling his very decline, it was superb. Venables had been able to get the best out of Gazza, and that impressed me too. Now, I was looking forward to working with 'El Tel'.

Venables had all the pizazz and chutzpah of the nightclub crooner he'd once been. When he arrived at Fratton as a 'consultant' in the summer of 1996 he was still adored by the English public and he brought a certain feel-good buzz to the team. Our first meeting with him as a Portsmouth team was in Stavanger in Norway, where we were based for pre-season. The trip to Stavanger was arduous: coach-boat-coach-boat-coach. When we arrived, many hours later, we were all exhausted. Then, out of nowhere, we heard the low rumbling of an airplane propeller, followed by the graceful landing of a seaplane, cutting smoothly across the blue fjord waters before coming to a halt. And out stepped 'El Tel', tanned, pearly white teeth beaming in the Norwegian sunshine, looking a million dollars after his plane journey.

Venables – who would go on to buy Portsmouth for £1 in February 1997 – proved something of a hindrance to Fenwick's authority, even if he was a welcome breath of fresh air. At half time during a match in Norway, Fenwick pulled me aside and scolded me for playing a ball to our right winger, Paul Hall. Instead, he wanted me to gather the ball in midfield before passing back to our full-back, building the move from deep. I protested. Why not just play the first ball? Why did I need to kill an attack by playing it to the full-back? By this stage, tempers had flared a little. Then, out of the shadows of the changing room, stepped Venables. 'He's right, Terry' he told Fenwick. I felt vindicated. At the same time, Venables had cut across Fenwick's authority; he should really have waited until after the game to have a quiet word with the manager. I felt a little for Terry Fenwick, in that regard, and all the more so since I've moved into the coaching and management of players myself. It was his first managerial appointment, and it was a big one. Despite our run-ins, I respected him as a very good coach and overall he treated me well. Ultimately, he was unlucky at Pompey. He could have done without Terry Venables undermining him.

The Venables factor meant that Pompey's FA Cup run of 1996-97 earned quite a bit of media attention. In a fifth round tie against Leeds United at Elland Road I scored the opening goal in a 3-2 victory which resulted in George Graham getting the sack and my old Ireland team mate David O'Leary taking over. In scoring, I picked up a bad injury. I could see I would get to the ball first but saw Leeds goalie Nigel Martyn charging at me. I knew that if I connected with the ball, he'd wallop me. I nodded the ball into the net and, sure enough, Martyn immediately clattered into me, smashing into my leg. Thanks to the adrenalin, I ran to the Pompey fans in celebration, before collapsing in pain with a dead leg. Poor Deby had travelled all the way up to Leeds to join my Mum and Dad in watching me play that day and arrived in the stadium just in time to see me being stretchered off. Spotting her in the crowd, I waved up to her while lying back on the stretcher, only with her to respond with a 'V' sign! Little did I know that she'd had a terrible journey. I hadn't given her very good instructions about how to get to Elland Road. Unable to find parking space before the game, she'd parked the car at the hotel, only to realise kick-off was fast approaching. She'd been offered a lift by a white van full of boozed up Pompey fans, only too happy to oblige a pretty young woman looking for Elland Road. She'd shared a bumpy, sweaty journey with eight Pompey lads, only to arrive at the ground just in time to see me being carted off.

After that win, Pompey were drawn at home against Chelsea in the quarter final. The day before, Terry Venables took the training session, discussing Chelsea's attacking threats such as Mark Hughes and Gianfranco Zola. Then he said something which I found hard to believe. 'Let Frank Leboeuf have the ball', he urged us. I looked at Paul Walsh, our striker, and he looked back at me. We were both waiting for him to elaborate. 'Leboeuf can't pass it', claimed Venables, 'so just give let him have the ball and he'll give it away'. I looked at Walshie again. Neither of us could believe what we were hearing. 'I beg to differ, Terry' I said; 'do you mean Frank Sinclair?' asked Walshie. But no, Venables meant Lebeouf. Just to be clear, this is the same Frank Leboeuf who marked Ronaldo out of the 1998 World Cup final, the same Leboeuf renowned for his incisive passes. The next day, finding ourselves 2-0 down against Chelsea, with Leboeuf effortlessly stroking the ball around Fratton Park as if it was a Sunday afternoon kick-about, I decided that enough was enough and on the way out of the tunnel at half time I told the lads to ignore what Venables had said. Deon Burton grabbed us a goal back but we ended up losing the tie 4-1. Chelsea went on to lift the cup that year, with Leboeuf commanding the final.

Pompey narrowly missed out on the play-offs to the Premier League that year, finishing seventh. The new season in 1997 brought a return to Maine Road, where I'd stood as a kid alongside Noel Gallagher and friends. Pompey were playing Manchester City in the first match of the First Division season. Oasis were charting strongly with 'Stand By Me' at the time and before kick-off Liam and Noel Gallagher came out during the warm up and started to bait the Pompey fans. Confronted by a swaggering Liam, the ever-vocal Pompey support responded in kind. Liam gave as good as he received, 'giving it large' to the Pompey fans, standing up and inviting several thousand of them to fight him. While all this was going on, I was doing my best to shelter from the heat on what was one of the warmest opening days of the season for many a year. Meanwhile, I think the Pompey fans were winning the battle of the banter and the

Gallagher brothers needed to find a response. Then, Noel spotted me. He sprinted over and jumped on me and, as I emerged from his grip, very publicly bear-hugged me. It was the first time I'd seen him since school and it was good to catch up. I doubt the travelling Pompey fans had any idea of our schoolboy past and must have found it all quite perplexing. On the pitch, the game finished 2-2. Straight after the final whistle, Noel invited me and Debs up to join the fun in the Gallaghers' private box where, evidently, the craic was mighty and all sorts of substances were flowing. Ever the conscientious pro, I declined. Roy Keane has a special term for people flaunting their celebrity, seeking to piggy-back on others' celebrity, or simply being over-friendly when such behaviour is not warranted: 'busy'. Joining Noel and Liam up there would have been just that: 'busy' behaviour. Just as it would have been had I 'spilled the beans' on what Noel was like at school, as several tabloid journalists were now begging me to. After seeing Noel and I embrace on the pitch, two redtop newspapers offered me very good money to provide them with an 'exclusive' on Noel's childhood. That really would have been the height of 'busy' behaviour.

With true friends, acting in what Roy Keane would call a 'busy' manner is not part of the deal. It was around this time that I first met a true friend and my best mate to this day, Lee. Portsmouth were playing Swindon in an away fixture at the County Ground. This was obviously a big game for me and a chance for Deby to mark the occasion with family and friends. Pompey won one-nil and I scored the winning goal (I've seen it since and I was actually offside, but hey, ho). That evening we headed out en masse to an Italian restaurant, where Deby and I found ourselves sitting opposite Lee, a Swindon Town season ticket holder, and his partner Shelly who was from my part of the country: Glossop, near Manchester. We struck it off immediately and remained friends from that day forth. In the years to come we holidayed together as couples and we grew close to their three children: Simone, Ava and Bryce. Shelly and Lee would remain a close part of my life and Lee, in particular, would prove a rock for me in some very testing times to come.

From Big Jack to Mick

In February 1996 Jack Charlton was replaced as Ireland boss by Mick McCarthy. My first encounter with Mick, after replacing Gary Waddock in 1990, had not been friendly. Since then, however, I'd learnt to deal with Mick's occasionally blunt manner and he'd apologised to me for the initial cold shoulder. Mick might come across as dour, but he has humility and the common touch as well as a lively sense of humour. That marks him out as a great man and is why he was able to become a great manager. After retiring from international football, he had taken charge of Millwall. I'd played against Mick's Millwall for Pompey and found them a very good passing side, not afraid to knock the ball about and play possession football. What really impressed me about Mick's managerial style was that he had been a rough and tough centre half in his playing days. Hardly a slick passer himself, he would bully you as a midfielder into doing some of his hard work for him. While he could be relied upon to cut out anything coming his way, possession football was hardly his trademark. I didn't think that Mick would take this managerial style with him into the Ireland job, but I was to be pleasantly surprised, in fact, shocked, at his bravery in taking this approach through to international level. Mick's Republic of Ireland team, unlike Jack's, was all about patient build up from the back, thought and purpose on the ball, and allowing players to express themselves.

If the winds of change were blowing thanks to the managerial transition, upstairs in the FAI change was also afoot. In the months following Jack's exit, there had been a series of crisis meetings and resignations at Merrion Square. Seán Connolly, our chief executive who'd lost his passport in Liechtenstein, was soon out of there, accompanied by a few of the other suits who'd been constants of the set up during the Charlton era. There were clearly deep divisions in the administrative structure which were disruptive enough for Mick but, from a player's perspective, I was happy enough to let the FAI carry out their very own Night of the Long Knives on their own terms. Post-purge, I just hoped that the new men would treat the players with a bit more respect, and carry themselves with a little less elitist swagger, than had previously been the case.

Needless to say, Mick's style suited my game a lot better than Jack's had. When Mick became national team manager, he brought me back into the fold and I blossomed under his management style, which was authoritative rather than authoritarian, and his coaching manner, which was enthusiastic and imaginative. Mick's appointment signified a bridge between the past and the future. He was a clear link to the Charlton years. After all, he was Jack's 'Captain Fantastic'. But he also brought in new blood, which was brave in itself. In March 1996, against Russia, he gave Shay Given his first cap and Roy Keane his first international captain's arm band, and introduced to the squad stars of the future like Damien Duff. The mingling of the senior players with the new crop was a success under Mick and in August 1996, in the first game in the qualifying campaign for the 1998 World Cup in France, I completed my first full ninety minutes for Ireland as we consigned the ghosts of the past to history by beating Liechtenstein 5-0. It was my twenty-fourth cap for my country.

And yet my relationship with Mick, which had improved immeasurably since his reaction to the Waddock exit in 1990, was almost jeopardised by some tomfoolery from within the squad. The annual FAI Player of the Year awards were always a ceremonial black-tie occasion and with the transition in management from Jack to Mick there was a strong attendance at that year's event. Rather a stiff occasion, place names indicated where one was to sit. But Steve Staunton, lurking around the hotel armed with a felt-tip pen, was up to no good. Mischievously, he had entered the room prior to the ceremony, found the manager's seat, and changed 'Mick McCarthy' to 'Mick McCarthorse'. When we filed in later, Mick was confronted with his new name. It brought all the old accusations about his robust and uncultured playing style flooding back. He was livid. 'Who did this?' He demanded of us. Stan, looking guilty, pointed at me. 'Cheers Stan!' I said. He had completely stitched me up. Mick just looked at me, shook his head, and took his seat. I was speechless. Mick didn't talk to me for the rest of the night. The following day there was no improvement in his mood so I had to explain to him that the prank had not been mine.

Roy Keane has since criticised Mick McCarthy for his poor man management. In particular, Paul McGrath's drinking was again becoming something of a problem and, in 1996, Mick insisted Paul join us at a Bryan Adams concert. I didn't really know where we were off to on that jaunt and I remember standing at the bar alongside Paul at that concert, out of view of the stage, when I had my very own Jason McAteer moment, remarking to him that the music sounded almost so good you'd think it was live. Paul, like everyone else, was lashing into the drinks and so my silly remark passed him by and spared me a ribbing from the lads. Looking at Paul, my relief at him ignoring my gaffe soon turned to pity. I realised that he wasn't there to enjoy a few sociable drinks with his fellow players; on the contrary, he was very efficiently going about the business of utterly anaesthetising himself in alcohol. Paul, knowing he would drink too much, hadn't wanted to go to the gig, but was persuaded to come by Mick in the interests of teambuilding, and ended up (predictably enough) getting shitfaced.

Now, I can see Roy's point. Paul McGrath's drink problem could and should have been managed more effectively. But at the same time, I think it's a bit unfair to hold Mick accountable for that one. Mick was trying to build a new team who would play a new style of football. To do so, he was throwing youth in alongside experience and, for that to work, he needed a team spirit akin to the winning energy around the place during the Charlton years. Mick wanted us to gel as a squad, to socialise together, to build a comparable team spirit. And in dealing with the brilliant, enigmatic talent that is Paul McGrath, he had two choices. He could either treat him as a man, trusting him to look after himself. Or he could exclude Paul, as had been the case during Jack's regime. Often, under Jack, poor old Paul would end up sitting on the bus on his own or else Mick Byrne would perform sentry duty, sitting outside his hotel room, solemnly turning away the drinks from the bar that Paul would order up. Paul was effectively held captive on more than one occasion under Jack's leadership. I love Paul and I know all about his troubled relationship with drink from first-hand experience, but it's a tough one and I wouldn't point the finger of blame at Mick McCarthy for poor man management. Quite the opposite, in fact.

Mick still retained the special team spirit honed under Jack, it was just that (by contrast to Jack) 'we love you Micky, we do, we love you Micky, we do' was never going to earn us a stop at a pub on the way back from our training base at the Nuremore Hotel in County Monaghan.

I was a constant in the Irish midfield for that 1998 World Cup qualifying campaign, playing in all ten matches; although I was now entering my thirties, Mick's managerial style at last allowed me the opportunity to put in some of my best international displays. In our first competitive match at home under Mick we comfortably beat Macedonia 3-0, before having to settle for 0-0 in our next home fixture, against Iceland. Unfortunately, failing to beat Iceland at home was to prove our undoing in that campaign. After that, we faced a tricky tie away to Macedonia. Mick went with experience, starting me, Roy Keane, Jason McAteer, and Andy Townsend across the middle and I gave us the lead, scoring after just eight minutes. The joy of scoring my second international goal was short-lived, however. We threw the lead away and Jason McAteer ended up getting sent off as we crashed to a 3-2 defeat. Our toughest game would be against Romania in Bucharest where Roy Keane missed a penalty and, with that, ended the realistic possibility of Ireland topping the qualifying group. Having picked up a booking in the previous game, I missed the Romania match and, as a result, did not play. It was all the more frustrating since I was our first choice penalty taker. Roy's miss had come as he deputised for me. Ireland recovered with comprehensive wins in the return fixtures against Iceland and Liechtenstein and beat Lithuania in Vilnius. Unfortunately, hopes of automatic qualification were now slipping away from us and, after drawing against 1-1 against Romania at a packed Lansdowne Road, we were again consigned to a play-off, this time against Belgium. In such high-stake games, a lone genius is often the difference between two evenly-matched sides. And so Belgian goal poacher Luc Nilis was to prove our bogeyman and our undoing over the two legs. Belgium were all over us for the first half hour of the home leg and Nilis hit the net for them in Dublin as we played out an unconvincing 1-1 draw. Then he went on to score the winner in Brussels, which meant that we lost by an aggregate of 3-2 over the two legs.

The failure to reach the 1998 World Cup was a real disappointment and brought emotions as hideous as the colour scheme of our orange away strip. I'd enjoyed playing alongside Roy Keane in midfield and we'd built up a good rapport. But when Roy had suffered a knee injury, I'd had to really step up to prove myself. To prove I could do it in midfield without Roy. To prove that I could steer the ship from midfield in a team undergoing a lot of personnel changes. To be a rock for Mick as he tried to work in the younger players. And I did. I received confirmation of this when I received the Irish Football Writers' Player of the Year for 1996. That award is a source of great pride to me. The Waterford Crystal trophy, shaped like a football, has pride of place in my study to this day. Justifying my starting place for Ireland was a personal victory, therefore. But it was also a pyrrhic one. The failure to qualify for the World Cup was a crushing blow. I knew that it was the last chance I would get to taste the World Cup finals, as I had done in 1990 and 1994. More than that, I wanted to eclipse the memory of Windsor Park in 1993. As strange as that sounds, I didn't want to be the hero after coming on for a mere twenty five minutes of a qualifying campaign and scoring a goal. I wanted to be regular, reliable Alan McLoughlin – not the fleeting hero, but the first team midfield stalwart that played every game and grafted away for qualification. It was as if, having played all the games of that campaign, I finally realised the fickleness of the five minutes of fame that had come that night in Belfast in November, 1993. It was time for someone else to step up and be the hero. But it wasn't to be. It's the first time I've been really upset by football and I'm not ashamed to admit that Ireland's failure to get to the World Cup in 1998 hurt one hell of a lot.

Portsmouth's centenary season of 1998-1999 was to bring similar lows. Terry Fenwick had been replaced by Alan Ball, the diminutive ginger-haired World Cup winner alongside Big Jack in 1966, and now back at the club for his second spell of management after taking Pompey to the top tier of English football in the '80s. Off the field, though, things were dire. The club was undergoing a serious financial crisis and, after being threatened by fans, chairman Martin Gregory sold his 97% stake, plunging the club into receivership. Pompey survived that year by a whisker, staying in the First Division only due to goal difference after a frantic final day of the season. Terry Venables was, by this stage, long gone, and a new owner emerged in the redoubtable shape of Serbian moneybags Milan Mandaric.

Mandaric, a Serb who had made his money in Silicon Valley, came onto the scene at Pompey in May 1999. Coincidentally, at the time the majority of Ireland's qualifiers for the European Championships of 2000 were taking place in the troubled corner of Europe from which Mandaric hailed. In our first game of that campaign we convincingly dispatched Malta 5-0 at Lansdowne Road. I was started in midfield for the next game, which would be an altogether tougher encounter, against Yugoslavia. Before flying out to that encounter, the players were asked individually (and confidentially) how they felt about travelling to Belgrade. The disintegration of the socialist Yugoslav state in the early 1990s had brought with it genocide and the mass displacement of populations. With ethno-national tensions in the region spilling over into horrific violence, everyone in the Ireland set-up was conscious of the fact that we would be entering what was effectively a warzone. As the team bus trundled from the airport to the hotel, I looked out the windows at collapsed walls, peeling plasterwork and wrecked buildings. A few months later, NATO air strikes would inflict further destruction on this grand old city. It was dark, crumbling and miserable. The next evening was a bitterly cold night, but we were given a warm welcome by the Partizan Belgrade Ultras, a jackbooted mob who made up the greatest proportion of a very hostile crowd of fifty thousand. Even the police joined in, whacking the Irish players on the calves with their truncheons as we lined up in the tunnel, ostensibly to get us moving onto the pitch for our own safety, but actually in a show of brute force. Behind Istanbul and Belfast (and of course, the 'Scummer' reception at Fratton Park) it was the greatest hostility I've faced as a professional. We ended up losing the game 1-0.

I played in our next match, a 2-0 home friendly triumph against Paraguay, and in a charity game against Northern Ireland at Lansdowne Road which followed. The match had been organised to raise funds for the victims of the Omagh bombing of 1998, in which 29 people were killed after a car bomb planted by dissident republicans exploded. It was a reminder that however bad things were in the Balkans, we still had our own problems at home. I didn't feature in our next two home games in that qualifying campaign, against Macedonia and Yugoslavia, but returned for the tie against Croatia in Zagreb, picking up a booking in a tight game in which Davor Suker poked home a Croatian winner in the ninety-fourth minute. The Croats had returned from the 1998 World Cup with their heads held high after finishing an incredible third in the world and yet there was nothing between the teams that day. The atmosphere in Zagreb was, similar to Belgrade, one of fervid, fiery nationalism. It was clear that the situation in the Balkans was rapidly deteriorating and with the Kosovo crisis unfurling in all its misery, politics once again started to encroach on the football. Not wanting to hand the Serbs the publicity of recognition after revelations about atrocities in Kosovo, the Yugoslav team travelled to Dublin only to be denied an official reception and the flying of their flag. Mick McCarthy spoke out about the moral dilemma facing us players as our away matches suffered postponement after postponement. The FAI even tried (unsuccessfully) to have our defeat in Belgrade wiped from the slate.

By this stage, our fixtures were concertinaing. The qualifiers brought disruption to everyone's plans and impacted hard upon family life. The postponements earlier in the competition meant that Ireland were forced into a quick succession of matches as, time running out, UEFA desperately tried to fulfil all the fixtures. For me, it meant changing plans I had made with Deby and the kids as Dad regularly set off for foreign fields. The weariness started to show as we laboured a 3-2 victory in our next game in searing Maltese heat, to put us within a hair's breadth of qualification. Next up, it was back to the Balkans, with a trip to play Macedonia in Skopje. We travelled there knowing that a victory would catapult us into Euro 2000 automatically. Promisingly, Niall Quinn put Ireland into the lead after just eighteen minutes. After a corner and a goalmouth scramble, Quinny, sitting on the turf, managed to hook the ball in their net with one of his Inspector Gadget-esque limbs. Agonisingly, after hanging on to our lead for over an hour, their equaliser came within seconds of the final whistle. After Alan Kelly had made a wonderful save, tipping the ball round our post, the Macedonian corner looped in, none of our players met the ball, and one of their players headed the ball goal-wards. We'd blown it, and now a playoff beckoned.

I knew that was that. Travelling home after that game, the mood was sombre. I had told Mick McCarthy at the start of the campaign that, aged thirty-two and going on thirty-three, this would be my last campaign with the Republic. After amassing forty-two caps I knew that the end was nigh. I felt numb when on the team coach and plane and then, after I returned home, the upset hit me. Shuffling into the house in the early wee hours of the morning, Deby could see I was down. As I sat on the bed, she sat down beside me and gave me a big hug. And that's when I let my guard down and football finally got the better of me. I cried with disappointment, a realisation that my time with Ireland was just about up, added to the feelings of failure for not qualifying. I also knew my international carrier was at an end. The Balkans had fallen apart and so had our qualifying campaign. Ireland lost the subsequent two-legged playoff against Turkey on goal difference. But the draw in Macedonia had been the decisive moment. After that match, I was pictured in the newspapers on my knees beneath the headline 'the face of anguish'. Those words barely did justice to the sense of disappointment

Back at Fratton Park, the mood was little better. A few months after arriving at Portsmouth and installing himself as chairman, Milan Mandaric came to see us at Woodbury Park, our pre-season training base in Nigel Mansell's property just outside Exeter in Devon. He summoned all the playing and coaching staff to a meeting. Mandaric may have been a Serb (not the most popular nationality in Europe at that time) but he looked, and acted, like a Wall Street CEO. The meeting in his office was actually nothing of the sort since the term implies, at the very least, a two-way conversation. Instead of a plural discussion, this was nothing less than a one-way dressing down with no dissent tolerated. It was American boardroom from start to abrupt finish. Looking towards the 1999-2000 season, he outlined his uncompromising vision for getting the club into the Premiership. If we were not in the top six by Christmas, he threatened, everyone would be getting the sack. Turning to Alan Ball, he announced dourly, 'and that includes you'.

With the sword of Damocles hanging over us, the players had a nervous close-season. Encamped at Woodbury Park, I tried to relax by hitting the golf course. One day I was enjoying a few rounds with my Pompey club-mate and card-carrying Scouser John Durnin, a man known as 'Johnny Lager' to the fans. Returning to the clubhouse we met the manager, who asked us if we'd seen Nigel Mansell's palatial house while completing our round. 'No' we replied. 'You must have gone a different route', he explained, and told us where to go in order to see Mansell's mansion. 'Here, take my buggy, it's a lot faster than the ordinary ones'. We thanked him and zoomed off, John Durnin on the left, driving, our teammate Adrian Whitbread on the right, and me sandwiched in the middle. Zipping along in the buggy, and with our eyes peeled for Mansell's gaffe, suddenly a ravine loomed. John, who hadn't been looking where he was going and was driving a bit too fast, swerved. As the buggy crashed I let out a scream. John baled out left, Adrian right, but I didn't have time to escape. The vehicle pitched up on its side, bending in half as it did so, and slicing into my skull. I went through the windscreen and emerged bloodied and in pain. I looked over to Whitbread, who was unscathed. I then looked over to John, who was grimacing in pain and clutching his elbow. Later he discovered that he'd dislocated the elbow and would be out for six weeks. My head gash required six stitches.

I thereby joined the glittering list of stupid footballer injuries. It wasn't quite as bad as goalkeeper Dave Beasant's infamous injury sustained when he dropped a tub of salad cream on his foot, but it wasn't far off. It was a genuine accident and not the result of us messing about, but I'm sure our chairman, Milan Mandaric, was none too pleased when he saw the madcap incident splashed across the papers the next day on what must have been an incredibly slow news day. Next morning at breakfast the club manager presented me with a bill: £175 for damage to the buggy and £135 for 'shrubbery damage'. As it was his personal buggy and since, at his urging, it had been overloaded with three people, I told him exactly what he could do with his bill. The golf buggy debacle was not to be the last of my daft injuries, though. Training with Pompey one day I fell against the post, bending my thumb back and, unbeknownst to me, causing me ligament damage. At home that afternoon, I was still nursing my sore thumb while trying to rock my baby daughter Megan to sleep in her little baby chair. After little success, I had to take a toilet break and didn't want to undo all my good work thus far. So I took Megan with me, still rocking her, while I sat down on the loo. I picked Megan up in her rocker again and, in this attempt at multi-tasking, managed to sever the remaining ligament (which had been hanging on for dear life after the incident in training). The resulting operation on my thumb put me out of action for three weeks. After the cancer diagnosis in 2012, I looked back on those couple of daft injuries, remembered how annoyed they'd made me at the time, and shook my head. Oh, how I would have swapped cancer of the kidney for the trifling matter of a scalp abrasion or a thumb ligament injury!

Perhaps the injuries were a metaphor for my club's misfiring form and my career's inevitable downward slide. With Pompey hovering dangerously close to the relegation zone after the first dozen or so games of the 1999-2000 season, Alan Ball knew the writing was on the wall. He called me into his office for a meeting and told me that he was getting the sack soon and that his assistant Kevin Bond was for the high-jump too. Ball told me that I was the club's only valuable asset, even aged thirty-three, and so I would have to be sold. 'Don't expect to be here next week', Ball told me. 'Expect to be in Wigan'. 'I'm not going to Wigan' I replied with the same resolve as if someone had offered me two years in a Siberian gulag. I had eighteen months left on my contract and that included my testimonial, the final curtain of a professional footballer's career. Ball had previously promised me a testimonial. A benefit game was in my Pompey contract, but he had said I deserved more than that after the amount of games I had played and the loyalty I had shown the club. As I reminded him of this, he just looked at me helplessly.

Back to the start again. Back to Swindon and the off-field financial failures that meant I had to move clubs against my wishes. Back to the sense of powerlessness. Back to the resentment at people making decisions over my head.

Only this time, I was at the other end of my career. Instead of being sold to a top team and having the World Cup to look forward to, I was being sold to Wigan – a small team – and as for the World Cup, or even the European Championship, well those had gone for a burton too. At Fratton Park, it was clear that an exodus was well underway. Knowing he was due the sack, Pompey assistant manager Kevin Bond was tapping up talent for Wigan, where his father John was assistant manager. That meant me. I demanded to meet with Mandaric, but he refused to meet me or even take a call. Again and again, I called, only to be told that Mr Mandaric was not available. I got angrier and angrier. I had given Pompey the best part of ten years. 309 league appearances. 54 league goals. Including cup games, 361 appearances in total. And 68 goals. Pompey had bought me for £400,000 and were selling me for £240,000. All that I'd given them had only cost them £160,000 in transfer fees. I didn't deserve this. But no one from the club would even do me the dignity of speaking with me. Of letting me down gently. Or harshly. Whatever. Anything was better than the rudeness of silence.

To make matters all the worse, I had just moved my family into our dream home in Warsash, an idyllic village on the river Hamble, not far from Portsmouth. I wanted to spend the rest of my career at Pompey, settle on the south coast, and go into coaching with the club. Now, it seemed, that dream was shattered. Worse still, faced with the prospect of moving to Wigan, Deby put her foot down. Exasperated that her dream move was off, she drew a line in the sand. She had put up with enough moves over the years and had had enough of my working life dictating all our moves as a couple. For some reason she did not find Wigan, located in the industrial north and famed for its pies and non-existent pier, enticing. I could go, if I had to. But she was moving back to Swindon. To her family. To her town. It now seemed that my career, not to mention my marriage, was teetering on the brink.

7

Losing a Kidney, Joining A Revolution

I WAS transferred from Portsmouth to Wigan Athletic at the turn of the millennium. The move didn't work for me on a number of levels. The first was the fact that the JJB Stadium just wasn't Fratton Park. Shiny and new, it lacked the charm and spirit of Fratton Park. It was also a step down a division and I missed the passion and the intensity of a big home following and all that brings to the footballing experience.

Still, I tried to put all that behind me and do my best in a Wigan shirt and the team won their first five games after I signed. I met some great people up there. Roy Carroll, later to become Manchester United goalie, was a space cadet but a great lad. Likewise Roberto Martinez, whom I played alongside in midfield, and got on well with. Due to the suddenness of the move, I was back living with Mum and Dad in Manchester and that meant we got to make up for all the years we'd missed when I was away playing football from a young age. I spent more time with my sister Diane, which was lovely, and I got to see my Nan before she died, aged 98 and just shy of her centenary. Nan probably sensed that all was not what I wanted it to be in my world, and calmed me down with her serenity and common sense. Here was a woman who'd seen it all, living through a revolution and the founding of a new state – born a subject of the Crown, becoming a citizen of the Republic – before emigrating to a new life in England. She reinforced for me the fact that, in my search for justification – for club, for country, for family – I had to take the rough with the smooth.

Nan's stoicism helped me through a big fall out with the Wigan chairman, Dave Whelan, the JJB Sports magnate, who was bankrolling the club. We were playing Colchester United one evening in a televised match. I was playing alongside Roberto Martinez in midfield and midway through the second half Roberto went down injured, causing a lull in play. I looked over to the Wigan main stand and caught a glimpse of the chairman, Whelan, hurriedly making his way from the director's box, down the steps, and over to the manager, John Benson, who was sitting in the stands with his assistant John Bond. I saw Whelan, dressed in his black chairman's overcoat, jabbing his finger towards Benson as he shouted directions into his ear. The next thing I know, Benson pulled out his phone and sent a call down to the bench. Next, my number appeared and off I trotted, none too pleased. When I reached the subs' bench, the manager, Benson, now down in the dugout, started giving me an earful. I looked back at him, seeing through his words. 'And who exactly is calling the shots here, John? You or the chairman?' That shut Benson up momentarily, but worse was to come.

Ten games into my Wigan career, in a match against Bristol Rovers, I slipped a disc in my lower back. As anyone who has suffered that injury knows, it brought excruciating pain. I staggered into training on the Monday afternoon after the injury, to find chairman Whelan paying his usual weekly visit. He strolled into the physio's room and, seeing me struggling with the pain, enquired 'what's up with you?

'I'm hurt bad, Mr Chairman,' I replied.

'It can't be that bad, can it?' he responded. 'I've just spent two hundred and sixty grand on you and I don't expect you to be lying on a treatment table.'

'Well, I know my body and I think it is that bad, Mr Chairman,' I retorted.

Club physio Alex Cribley then pitched in, telling Whelan that I would require a scan.

'I'm not paying for a scan,' Whelan shot back snappily.

It took me a few moments to process this remark before registering the implication.

'What? Don't you believe me?' I asked him, incredulous.

Whelan was silent. Then I felt the anger start to rise in me. The same anger that had caused me to lash out at Joe Royle as a lad. What was he trying to say?

'You think I'm faking it, don't you?' I demanded. 'In all my playing career no one has ever called me a cheat before. This is a first. How dare you?'

Whelan appeared shocked and turned on his heels. As he left the room he instructed Cribley to go ahead with the scan. 'If there's nothing wrong, he can pay for it,' he told him; 'if there is, the club'll pick up the bill'. Like all cynics, Whelan knew the price of everything but the value of nothing. He just could not believe that he'd splashed a quarter of a million pounds on a player who was now injured. But, finding myself on the wrong end of his implication, I didn't hold back. After all I'd been through in my career, representing club and country dutifully for years, I considered his suggestion the lowest that could have been levelled at me. If he'd accused me of not giving my all in a certain game, I'd have argued the toss, but to hint that I was faking injury was simply outrageous.

My slipped disc certainly was genuine, so much so that it ruled me out for three months. My return game was a match against Bournemouth, the last match of the season, with Wigan now in the throes of a playoff push. I shouldn't have played and by half time I knew it. Since returning to fitness, I had only gone through two training sessions and forty-five minutes in a reserve game. I was blowing out of my arse, not yet fully fit and, as a seasoned professional, old enough and wise enough to know this was the case. So at half time I told Benson to take me off for the good of the team. The news filtered back up to Whelan, which led to another run-in and the inevitable breakdown in the relationship. The chairman soon instructed his manager to drop me for the play-off semi-final and for all games thereafter. I was never to play for the club again, according to Whelan's order.

It was a blow, alright. How was I to respond? Shrug my shoulders, admit defeat, and leave the club? No way. I dug my heels in, gritted my teeth, and trained every day. I was at loggerheads with a chairman with a puffed ego but I wasn't at the stage of my career where I was willing to be pushed around. Dave Whelan is a respected businessman who brought Wigan from next to nothing to cup glory in 2013, for which he deserves much credit. But his rule also verged on the tyrannical. In the eighteen months I was with Wigan, they went through five managers. First Benson, then Bruce Rioch, then Steve Bruce, then Colin Greenall, then Paul Jewell. Whelan even slapped a ban on me talking to the local press. I remember scoring the 'golden goal' (after it had just been introduced) in an LDV Vans Trophy match against Oldham Athletic. The press milled around me and then, informed of the chairman's diktat by a single whispered word from a club mandarin, sloped away apologetically. It was as if everyone at the club was cowed by Whelan and the sheer pettiness of his approach started to really get to me. In the playoff final of 2000 against Gillingham I, along with a few others, was given a cup final suit but not even allowed to train with the first eleven and the substitutes on the Wembley turf before the match. That was an unnecessary slight. So me, Roberto Martinez and Dave Lee hopped on the tube from Wembley into London, dressed in our tracksuits and looking like three wannabe rappers headed for Covent Garden and a free-styling contest. Unlike Dave and Robbie, all I wanted to do was sink a few pints. We returned that evening to the hotel where, a few beers on me, I came across Benson and his coterie of sycophants and let fly. But that was the one and only occasion where I let my enmity with Wigan's senior management publicly spill over.

And yet the greatest factor behind my Wigan move turning sour, I realise now, was my distance from home. From Deby. From the girls. From emotional security and love. Debs had moved back to Swindon as soon as I had made the move up to Wigan. That was an incredibly hard decision which really tested our marriage. She understood why I had to make the move, of course. Footballers' pensions work on the basis of the best three consecutive years' earnings, multiplied by your years in the game, plus a payment from the football league. Earning more at Wigan than I was at Pompey, it made sense for me, for us, that I made the move in the twilight of my career. But it made for a very rocky eighteen months in our marriage. The kids were young, we were apart for long periods, and I really wasn't happy in my job. My international career had come to an end and I was lacking a lot in my life. We could have gone our separate ways at that point, and the thought of that horrifies me now. It was eighteen months of unhappiness, of Megan and Abby seeing their Dad infrequently, of telephone calls with so much left unsaid.

I should have been more patient in assessing my options when making an exit from Pompey. I should have taken more time. But I had been instrumental at Pompey for nine years, and I still was able to perform; the thought, at that stage, of a hiatus in my playing career – of taking a break from football, my life's work – was more than I could bear. I just had to be playing. On top of my love for the game, I had to play to be able to bring in the money to support my family. Football had come to define my life and my life's roles. I now realise that the in rush to perpetuate my relationship with football, I was jeopardising my marriage.

Back up north, Roy Keane provided a shoulder to cry on: metaphorically speaking, of course. Roy knew I was in the area and going through a tough patch with Wigan and invited me over to his leafy Cheshire home on a few occasions. I did not find Roy's hospitality of the 'busy' variety which he dreads; on the contrary, it was most welcome. We chatted about lots: the Ireland set-up over the years; the professional footballer's career options; my unhappy predicament at that time. Those conversations with Roy helped steel me for my showdown with Wigan Athletic. The club were bristling to get rid of me and I was ready to go. I had only turned out twelve or thirteen times for the club and I was becoming a liability for them, appearing in reserve games when promising teenagers should have been given their chance instead. Finally I was called in to meet the club secretary, Brenda Spence, and John Benson, now Director of Football. The club and I had agreed a settlement figure to mutually cancel my contract and, symbolically, I handed over my kit in return. The next day I arrived to pick up my farewell cheque which, to my disgust, amounted to about ten grand less than the figure agreed the day before. I grabbed my kit back and told Spence and Benson where to go. 'The chairman's on his way here' they countered, to which I replied that I didn't give a proverbial. Seeing that I was resolute, they flinched first. Together, before Dave Whelan arrived, we sorted out a compromise. I can't go into much more detail, but I got what I was owed. Stupidly, the fair and proper solution to the situation had to be sorted out behind the chairman's back.

I returned home, to Deby, to Megan and Abby, to Swindon and to family life. I was now in my mid-thirties but in my head I was that same restless teenager waiting for my first break in football: impatient, stroppy, frustrated by gnawing ambition. It was not long before I was itching to play football again. I was only home a couple of weeks before picking up the phone and speaking to Roy Evans, who was then the Swindon manager. I asked him if I could come and train. I even offered to play for free. The club were in financial difficulty and I knew that Roy didn't have the money to be splashing on a thirty-four year old, no matter his former standing at the club. I was so desperate to be close to Deby and Megan and Abby I think I would have paid to play if it had come down to it. I knew that for the fans the novelty of seeing a club favourite reappear for Swindon would soon wear off when it became apparent that my pace and stamina were not what they were when I was the club's Wembley hero. But I didn't care. I just wanted to make the move and start playing regular football again. Finally, Roy Evans agreed to sign me. Before long, though, he had received the sack from Swindon. I then got an offer from manager Colin Addison to play for Swansea, which is just about a manageable commute from Swindon, but which fell through. Things were starting to look desperate.

At this stage I had been home for two months and was living

off my farewell payment from Wigan. It was becoming increasingly clear to me that the end of the road was fast approaching. I was in my mid-thirties and had a recurrent injury problem. Soon, I would have to reconcile myself to life without football. It was a tremendously hard realisation to come to. Football fans, even armchair supporters, often talk about withdrawal symptoms at the end of a lengthy televised tournament or a league season. So you can imagine the depression that sets in after the end of a playing career. I now knew that the same emotions, multiplied a thousand times, were waiting just around the corner.

Then Rochdale came knocking in the shape of manager John Hollins. I was straight up with John, and I told him I could play until the end of the season, when I would be retiring. I knew it was time. What with my slipped disc, and with the family situation, I just couldn't manage another long stint in the North West. And so I played my last football league match for Rochdale against Bristol Rovers on 20 April 2002, when I scored a penalty with eight minutes to go. That was enough to see the club into the playoffs for the first time in their history and I was pleased to have done my small bit. But, for me, that was to be it. I'd made my football league debut on 12 September 1986 and my last league game was on my birthday, 20 April 2002. With that penalty I took my football league bow with 550 football league games and over 100 goals to my name. It was the day of my thirty-fifth birthday, and Mum and Dad were there to see my last league game, just as they had been there to see my first, all the way back in 1986.

Saipan and all that

I'd like to say that I settled happily into retirement, that just being at home with the wife and kids gave me all the fulfilment I needed. But I'd be telling a bare-faced lie. Neither did the golf course provide me with any sort of succour. Retirement from professional football is shit. Really shit. Simple as that. You're sat around at home for a week, enjoying the time off, enjoying the fact that you don't have to go in for training. Then, after about a week, it hits you. The boredom. The lack of male camaraderie. The lack of banter. The lack of purpose. You're left scratching your head, thinking 'this is nice, but I can't afford to retire full stop'. To keep my house, my family, my lifestyle, I couldn't just put my feet up. And yet all the time, you must come to terms with the fact that you can no longer perform your very trade. You can't put your feet up but neither can you earn money through your feet any longer. Aged just thirty something, you are already over the hill. It's awfully demoralising, it's tremendously deflating, and personal relationships suffer as a result. Some move on quickly. Some turn to booze. Some mope around the house. As Deby will attest, I was hard to live with for a while. I would watch football matches on television, envious of the fact that I would never play at that level again.

When Ireland reached the World Cup finals in 2002 I was on holiday in Greece with Deby, Abby and Megan. And then suddenly, spectacularly, disastrously, the McCarthy-Keane rivalry erupted in the infamous Saipan incident. The bust-up would divide Irish public opinion, some branding it the cause of a second civil war in Ireland. The facilities and general preparation on the isle of Saipan (Ireland's pre-tournament training base) had not met Roy's expectations and, after his disquiet was leaked to the press, Mick sent him home. This was sensational. Even the Taoiseach publicly urged both men to kiss and make up: to no avail. I picked up the phone and glanced through all my former

Republic of Ireland colleagues in the phone book. A journalist would kill for these contacts right now, I told myself. I was itching to find out what was going on, to be an integral part of the Ireland squad, as I had been for the best part of a decade. On the TV at the hotel bar I watched Niall Quinn and Steve Staunton appear alongside Mick at a press conference. What was going on? My good friend Alan Kelly was caught up in the middle of it all. He would have the inside track. I grabbed my mobile and thought about giving him a quick buzz. And then I thought better of it. I didn't want to act in any way that could be construed as gossipy or, as Roy, Mick McCarthy's bête noire, would have it put it, 'busy'. As a result, to this day – having heard both sides of the story many times from many people – I'm still not one hundred per cent sure I know what happened out there.

I had seen the first flaring-up of that legendary dispute in America in 1992. I had lived and breathed and sweated beside many of the men whom I watched on the big screen in a Greek hotel. And as Ireland battled out of the group, and went the distance with Spain in the second round, I willed them on passionately but silently, urging us to win, flinching from the agony of the penalty shoot-out defeat, all the while hidden at the back of a dark mass of British and Irish hotel guests. Hidden. Alone. Skulking at the back of the room. Truth is, I didn't want to show my face. I didn't want the inane conversations, the bar-room tactical 'wisdom'. I knew these players like they were my brothers. I didn't want to hear the opinions of lounge lizards and sun-burnt self-appointed football geniuses. I didn't want to hear this player or that player being slagged off: 'he's got to take off Kilbane' or 'what's Duff doing?' Nor, at the same time, did I want to share my pride in Mick's achievement with the team, or even my pain at Ireland's eventual elimination. I didn't want to howl in glory or curse in defeat with these people, these ordinary fans. I didn't want to be recognised. Why? Because not so long ago, that was me on the big screen. And that thought was almost too much to bear.

After we returned from that holiday, and after the embers of Saipan slowly burnt themselves out, I eventually pulled myself together and got my teeth into coaching. I should have taken my coaching badges earlier, but there was never time due to international duty. Now I had time on my side, so I threw myself at the task with determination. I also called Roy Keane, who at the time was under house arrest imposed by the media and besieged by paparazzi. I offered him, his wife Theresa, and their kids a bolt-hole: my house in Swindon. 'I'm not being busy, Roy' I assured him. 'I'm just grateful for you being there for me while I was at Wigan and I want to return the favour'. He thanked me heartily. It was a genuine offer amidst a veritable shit-storm of Roy's least favourite thing in the world – people being busy – and right outside his front door. Still, he didn't take me up on the offer. Deep down, I knew he wouldn't.

It was while earning my UEFA 'B' licence at St Albans that I bumped into Nigel Spink, then manager at Forest Green Rovers, a conference club situated in Nailsworth, Gloucestershire just twenty-eight miles from Swindon. I wanted to play football so I signed, but soon realised the folly of that idea. In a match at Barnet, I compounded my disc problem by prolapsing it. This new agony resulted in twelve days on the floor screaming in pain whenever I moved. If I so much as moved my neck I would be crippled by horrific pain shooting down my spinal cord to the very tips of my toes. I could pee from my stationary position on the floor, but getting up to go to the toilet meant shuddering pain. I was a physical wreck.

Ten weeks after the prolapse I had an epidural, which brought sudden and miraculous relief. An injection into the prolapsed disc seemed to really do the trick and, aged thirty-five, but with the vigour of Lazarus, I dared to think that I could still perform as a footballer. Returning to Forest Green to take a training session, I asked the groundsman if he could keep the lights on for an extra fifteen minutes after the session so I could do a couple of laps by myself and start to regain my fitness. Well, it was soon clear from the pain that I wasn't able to jog. A brisk, toe-curlingly painful walk was the extent of my recovery. I managed one lap and made my way into the changing room forlornly. And there I declared to the slightly bemused club physio, who was clearing away his things, that that was that. My footballing days were over. This time, well and truly over.

Unlike many retired professional footballers today, I have to work. I haven't pissed or gambled my money away like some, I just happened to retire just before the huge money started rolling in to English football. I've no grudges against players earning super salaries today, but the most money I ever earned as a footballer was a long way from the hundred grand a week packet some of the top players take home now. At Manchester United, Eric Harrison made everyone start a pension young and when I left Southampton I put the settlement money into that scheme. On top of that, however, I still have to earn a crust. I'm thankful that Mum and Dad instilled a work ethic in me because I've been something of a jack of all trades after hanging up my boots. One job was as a delivery man with Securicor in Swindon. On several occasions, I would walk onto the shop floor and see people turn around and clock who I was. 'Hello, Alan' they'd say, but I knew that they were really thinking to themselves 'Jesus, a Swindon million pound footballer has come to this'. That was difficult. Really difficult. After the first couple of times I even felt like donning a wig, a false moustache, or a sombrero with a droopy moustache so people wouldn't recognise me. 'Alan, is that you?' they'd ask. 'No, Señor' I could reply, and shuffle off unrecognised. But you just have to swallow your pride and get on with providing for your family. And so I made the transition from football into the 'real' world of work. Without a disguise and without letting my head drop. I helped as a removals man with my best friend Lee; became a quality controller at the local Honda factory; worked fifteen months in a printing company; and qualified as an NVQ tutor to young adults struggling to find employment. It was some transition but, like everything else that life has thrown at me, I just had to face up to it and get on with it.

Et tu, Keano?

Jack of all trades, master of none. Retirement from football was tough enough, but it did not brace me for a nasty encounter I had not seen coming. When Roy Keane's autobiography was published in 2002, I was shocked to read the following words describing the intensity of the pre-match atmosphere when we faced Northern Ireland in November 1993:

'Knowing little of the history, lads like Andy Townsend, John Aldridge, Tony Cascarino and Alan McLoughlin were puzzled.'

Now, Townsend and Aldridge may have qualified through the 'granny rule' and Cass, as he later revealed, had no immediate Irish heritage and wasn't actually entitled to an Irish cap at all. But me? Both my parents were Irish and had a good grasp of the nation's history; I knew exactly what that rivalry was all about. Just as much, if not more, than Roy Keane. Our friendship, which had first developed in Big Jack's Ireland squads, had deepened when I was at Wigan between 1999 and 2001. Deby had popped over to Roy's with me a couple of times and I had dined with Roy and his wife Theresa quite a bit. I often enjoyed walks with one of the most famous dogs in football: his beloved Triggs. But that line really angered me. It was as if Roy was taking something away from my achievement in scoring that night. As if the pictures of us embracing at the final whistle in Belfast in 1993, looking forward to America, had all been staged for the cameras.

I thought about calling him up and asking 'Roy, what's all this crap in the book?' In the end, I didn't have to. Roy called me one afternoon while on his way back from Sunderland. I was sitting at my desk in the printing company in Swindon when the call came, so it was a nice surprise. He explained that his ghost writer, Eamon Dunphy, had put a lot of words, those included, into the book.

That was Roy's explanation and I believe it. I have to. Roy was a fellow professional footballer, a colleague, a friend. But I was still seething about the passage. I had represented my country forty-two times; left my first child's birth to get on a plane to play football for Ireland; taken us to the World Cup; generated millions for the FAI; put up with crap hotels; numbed my arse on an Albanian bench; suffered death threats from Combat 18: you name it. That is why those words really niggled. It was as if, having wrecked my body playing for my country, I was still seeking justification.

Fast forward to 2012. A decade later. And the same old crap. It was no coincidence that Ireland were again appearing in their first big tournament since the World Cup in 2002. With excitement about the European Championship finals mounting in Ireland, I hit the road in Ireland with John Aldridge as part of a media gig, touring the country. And then, out of nowhere, I heard about Joey Barton's latest Twitter rant. Barton had reacted to a perceived slight from my former Republic of Ireland international colleague Matt Holland, as is his wont, by going completely overboard, saying 'if you're English, you play for England. If you're English and shit you pretend your Irish grandparentage matters to you and play for Ireland.' Matt, graciously, declined to respond. But to me Barton's tirade was old hat. My overwhelming feeling was that we'd heard this sort of intellectual laziness before and we'd go on to hear it all again. There was nothing original in what the self-proclaimed 'Philosopher King' of football had to say. But it was still out of order. I spoke to several Irish journalists who had picked up the story. I told them my honest opinion: that Barton is an uneducated person who spends more time concentrating on Twitter than improving his own game. Indeed, if Joey Barton had spent more time on his game and less on off-field rubbish, he could well have been capped by England more than once.

Just look at the other countries that do the same thing that Ireland do in recruiting second and third generation players: Italy, France, or Germany. In fact, England had a fantastic player who, in 1984, scored one of the best goals I have ever seen. I was 17 years old in 1984: national unemployment was at a high and police and picketers were clashing in the miners' strike. The mood of the country was summed up by a chart hit of that year by The Smiths, like me Manchester Irish lads – 'Heaven Knows I'm Miserable Now'. Then, totally unexpectedly, English fans were treated to a little bit of magic in the Rio de Janeiro sunshine. An English player showed the Brazilians how it was done by dribbling past no less than six players and the keeper before calmly slotting home. His name?

John Barnes. His birthplace? Kingston, Jamaica.

With football fever gripping Ireland in the run up to the 2012 championships, I had the chance to confront Eamon Dunphy about his ignorant remarks about English-born Irish players lacking a sense of history and identity. I was booked to appear on the Craig Doyle show on RTÉ but wasn't told who the other guests would be. As I entered the green room, to my surprise, I saw Dunphy. As we exchanged greetings I thought nothing of it. But then, after I'd settled on an armchair on the opposite side of the room to him, my mind wandered back to those comments in Roy's book. And then it wandered back further ...

I am fifteen years old, sitting beside Dad – a gentle yet principled man – in St Kent's social club in Manchester. We're enjoying the trad music when, through the fog of cigarette smoke, a collection bucket 'for the cause' is passed under our noses. 'You're not putting anything in there' Dad instructs me sharply as it comes to us, and he passes the vessel on.

I looked back to Dunphy and my eyes narrowed. Bloody hell, I thought, Eamon Dunphy is some man to be playing the patriot game. When Dunphy had written those words, he'd reduced Irishness to a simple formula and, in doing so, replicated exactly the sort of post-independence snobbery he is fond of railing against: an insular and small-minded attitude. But neither was it the right occasion to settle scores. Although tempted, I wasn't going to stomp over to Dunphy and demand a word. After all, we were there to talk about Ireland's chances in Euro 2012, not Windsor Park, 1993. The professional thing was to keep tight-lipped, which I did at the time, but I do hope that Eamon Dunphy gets to read these words. It seems like there's still a long way to go with the whole British-Irish thing and I've witnessed the worst of that spirit of loathing. It isn't healthy and it isn't nice. But then 2012 was to bring much greater worry for me than the damnable question of Anglo-Irish relations.

Madness at Pompey

Before the cancer diagnosis, I had made the move into radio punditry. In 2005, after impressing in a post-match interview at Fratton Park, I was invited to commentate on Portsmouth radio station The Quay. I was thrown in at the deep end: Pompey's tumultuous Premiership season 2004-2005, during which Harry Redknapp – the club's promotion winning manager just a season before – became pantomime villain after leaving the club and taking the manager's job at deadly rivals Southampton. Pompey walloped Southampton 4-1 in the dying throes of that league campaign and, knowing that a defeat on the final day against West Bromwich Albion would relegate Southampton, I commentated as my hero Bryan Robson's Baggies walked out 2-0 victors against a Pompey team that was barely lifting a leg in effort to keep their south coast rivals up. I would go on to do match commentary for Pompey games for four years, home and away. If anything, it was through the radio work that I fell back in love with Pompey, my club, and the fans. I tried to be as honest, as concise, as to-the-point as I could be, struggling to rein in my natural affinity with the club. My no-nonsense opinions soon ensured that I was once again earning a place in the Pompey fans' hearts and Quay radio's commentary soon resulted in a cult following for the station, resulting in the club eventually buying the station. On the back of that work I soon got slots on Talksport, where I still work doing the football feeds that go out around the world, and with Irish station Newstalk and BBC local radio.

As a radio pundit, I was well placed to analyse the extraordinary boom and subsequent bust of Portsmouth Football Club, a story which has become a chamber of horrors displaying the worst imaginable financial irresponsibility in football. Thanks to Milan Mandaric's money, Pompey were destined for the big time. After I'd left the club, Mandaric had gone on the hunt for a manager suited to his immense and ruthless ambition and finally found one in Harry Redknapp. Cockney 'Arry is a real football man, a clever wheeler-dealer and, whatever Pompey fans think about him now, he put together an impressive side that romped up to the Premiership as First Division champions in 2003 in his first season at the helm. The Fratton faithful were treated to the renaissance of experienced professionals like Teddy Sheringham, Paul Merson, Patrick Berger and Steve Stone, who played well together and played well for Redknapp. Promotion to the Premiership worked well for Pompey and Redknapp, whose formula kept on working. By the time I started radio commentary on Pompey games, the club was a respectable Premier League side. Redknapp had departed but was soon to return. There seemed no ceiling to Pompey's upward trajectory, no rude reality check which usually faces newly promoted clubs.

Mandaric, however, had had enough and – whether unwilling or unable to financially sustain the club's successes – he sold the club to Alexander 'Sacha' Gaydamak, a Russian-Israeli businessman with links to the arms trade. Eyebrows were raised over Gaydamak's suitability for the job, but no one spoke out too loudly. After all, he too was pouring money into the club and Pompey were soon attracting top players. The likes of Lassana Diarra, Sol Campbell and Jermaine Defoe were soon arriving at Fratton Park. Their salaries were enormous. I mentioned this at the time. I also drew attention to the fact that the boom was not sustainable. If Pompey were serious about sustaining their triumphs, they needed to build proper training facilities, invest wisely in the youth setup, and develop the stadium. On the one hand, I was striking a note of caution. On the other hand, I, just like everyone else, was spellbound by the magic of Pompey's rise. At the time, who cared too much about sustainability? Throw some more cash at the club, Mr Gaydamak. That's it. Ninety per cent of the club's income going on player's salaries? Don't worry about it. The stadium's falling to bits? No worries, we've vague plans for a shiny new one on the seafront. Throw some more petrol on the bonfire. Watch the flames rise!

And oh, how they rose! Pompey finished eighth in the Premier League and in 2008, under 'Arry, they won the FA Cup. It was the club's first silverware since winning back-to-back league titles between 1948 and 1950. While I was vocal in my criticism of the club for not building a proper training ground during the glory years, that was to prove the thin end of the wedge. What followed next was sickening for everyone associated with the great old club. Pompey enjoyed UEFA Cup football on the back of the cup success and I travelled to Portugal to cover an away fixture against Braga, getting totally carried away with the whole experience, rising as Peter Crouch did to nod in Pompey's goal and almost scrapping with a Portuguese counterpart who pulled one of our plugs out of its socket. Fratton Park was literally rocking for the visit of AC Milan during that UEFA Cup campaign, which ended in a 2-2 draw. I don't think I've ever heard such noise. The European football would prove a chimera, however. Gaydamak suddenly cut off the money supply in 2009. 2010 was a year of mixed [illegible] with Pompey plunged into administration and docked [illegible]s, effectively consigning them to relegation. Incredibly, [illegible] side made the FA Cup final again that year but lost narrowly to Chelsea. Like at Swindon, though, the club's fate had been sealed in the boardroom: by financial recklessness at the club itself and by the successive ten point deductions meted out by the FA as a consequence.

During the glory years at Fratton, I was interviewed by Portsmouth chief executive Peter Storrie with a view to managing the youth team at Pompey. This was in 2005 when French coach Alain Perrin had replaced Redknapp, before Harry returned to the club and guided Pompey to FA Cup victory. I was offered the job on the condition that I relocated to Portsmouth from Swindon. I love Portsmouth but I turned it down as both my girls were at school in Swindon and the move would have meant too much turmoil for them. Partly because I was away on foreign duty for so long when they were growing up, I wanted to be around more than ever and, as I explained to Peter, for me and Deby their education came first. I wasn't going to make the same mistake twice and imperil my marriage, my family life. I felt that I was being reasonable and offered to commute in from Swindon every day. I told Storrie that if he understood my terms, I'd be willing to chat again. If he had a problem, he could leave it. If not, he was to call me back in twenty minutes. He called again, twenty minutes later. Great, I thought, me remaining in Swindon was not an issue. So I travelled down to Fratton Park for the interview six days later. After the interview, I was told that I had the job. I was delighted. But then Storrie, incredibly, inserted the proviso again. He was still insisting that I relocate. 'I thought we went through this last week', I said. He could see I was annoyed. I told him that it was out of the question and so, as a sweetener, he even offered me half the first team bonuses if I would relocate. This would have been an attractive option if the team were winning at the time, but they weren't, so I told him to stick it up his arse. Ultimately, he had wasted my time.

In analysing the torrid tale of Pompey's recent rise and fall, our fans would be entitled to ask why Peter Storrie didn't shout 'stop' at some stage. Although the chairman and board at the time were also to blame, it was Storrie's responsibility to understand the economics of the situation. When you are getting just twenty thousand fans through the door on a match-day you can't be splurging seventy grand a week on this player or that player. The club should have invested in infrastructure during the good times, bought a proper training ground, improved Fratton Park, adding an extra ten thousand seats. But, much like Ireland during the Celtic Tiger boom, no one was thinking long term. Storrie was the man in day-to-day charge and Harry Redknapp, as manager, was always going to spend as much as he was given. Still, there's been an awful lot of hand-wringing going on after Pompey's fall from grace, and it's come from every quarter. I don't like that. Pompey's cup win in 2008 was fantastic but, quite frankly, that legacy has gone to rat shit. Storrie, as chief executive, was paid handsomely and needed to put the medium and long-term ahead of the short-term gain. The failure to do so almost led to the club sliding into the waters of the Solent for ever more. Harry Redknapp delivered results which the fans revelled in at the time, but surely Harry, too, must have realised that the club's ascent wasn't sustainable over a long period of time. It's easy to say 'I was just doing my job', but you also have to look around you when in a position like that. Be fair. Be realistic. And – above all – be responsible.

As Pompey teetered and fell, I was still performing commentary on radio. Just about. In the excitement of a Premiership game between Reading and Pompey, I'd mistakenly referred to Stephen Hunt as Stephen something-that-rhymes-with-Hunt. 'Sacked in the morning, you're getting sacked in the morning' was the cry around the press box that evening. Fortunately, I was let off with a warning. On another occasion, after Pablo Zabaleta went down theatrically in a game, I referred to him as a 'fairy' live on Ireland's Newstalk radio. That earned me another ticking off. In 2010, I was inducted into the Portsmouth FC Hall of Fame alongside the likes of Jimmy Dickinson, a man who played for England 48 times and Pompey a record 764 times. In firing Ireland to USA '94, I was the first Portsmouth player to be included in a World Cup squad since the great Dickinson had played in the 1958 tournament. Considering I had joined Pompey as a 'dirty Scummer', it was some achievement to make the club's Hall of Fame. That, and being inducted into Swindon's Hall of Fame, meant an awful lot to me.

My final couple of jobs before rejoining Pompey in June 2011 were both football-related. The penultimate one was at a printing firm in Swindon, where I produced the FA county magazines; the last one was as a tutor in the NVQ in Sports Recreation based around football to teenagers aged between 16 and 18. Football, so it seemed, was calling me back – calling me ever closer to a coaching role – until in 2011, my love for the club reaffirmed, I was brought back into the Pompey fold by my former playing colleague and then Academy manager Andy Awford, who made me Under 16s manager, after which I progressed to Senior Academy Coach. It meant giving up other radio commitments with the BBC, but it felt great to be back in the cut and thrust of everyday football. Events off the pitch, however, were soon threatening the very existence of the club, let alone my job. After subsequent changes in ownership, involving the usual comic opera carry-on of fake Sheikhs and tycoons with empty pockets, the club entered administration again in 2012, after the arrest of Pompey's new owner Vladimir Antonov for asset stripping. Antonov, a Lithuanian, left debts of over thirty million, plus owing seventeen million to the Hong Kong moneylender Balram Chainrai. It's astounding to think that the FA have a 'fit and proper person' test when football clubs are subject to takeover, which has been in place since 2004. It would seem that Lithuanian asset strippers are OK in their book. Unsurprisingly, with all this going on and with liquidation a realistic threat, the club was hurtling down the football league at a furious pace. The club's main appearances were now not on the pitch, but at the High Court in London. It looked like Portsmouth had been given a death sentence.

Battling Through

Devastatingly, at the same time, our good friends Lee and Shelly received some terrible news. Deby had called over to Shelly at her home and found her sitting on the stairs and not feeling well. Tests were carried out the at the hospital, where the scans revealed a cancerous growth on her brain. Shelly had suffered breast cancer previously and now, after three years in the clear, it had returned. Deby and I rallied around our friends as best we could. Shelly was determined to make it through. Lee was distraught. Their children were upset. We did everything we could to support them, but it was hard not to get dragged down by the sense of despair. It was my first encounter with the frightful misery of cancer. And it wouldn't be the last. In 2011 and 2012, as my club was spiralling downwards, so – unbeknownst to me – was my health, as a tumour on my kidney appeared and set about its malignant growth.

I don't know when the growth started, but it went undetected until that day in September 2012 when my cancer announced itself so spectacularly. The blood. The hospital visits. The panic. Then, the diagnosis.

Doctor Lacovou, in his snazzy linen suit, had just left the room. I had just apologised to him for having to break such terrible news. Shortly after the doctor left, Deby and my girls filed into the room, sheepishly. I then had to break the news to them. It was a dreadfully hard thing to do. Their rock, their provider, was seriously ill. Once again, I pitied Doctor Lacovou and all those like him, who have to break such news on a regular basis. I've spoken about how hard it was to break the news to my wife and kids, not to mention my Mum and Dad and sister Diane, but there was another person to whom it was probably even harder: my best mate, Lee, who'd just arrived in the hospital room.

Lee's wife Shelly was slowly slipping away from us, suffering from the same dreadful and aggressive disease which I had been newly diagnosed with. Knowing what he was going through made my situation all the worse. He just looked stunned, as if life shouldn't have to be full of such constant bad news. Deby, by contrast, was wailing 'No!', over and over again, in defiance of the diagnosis. As if roaring at my cancer would make it disappear. She had been nursing Shelly for the past year, watching her best friend gradually deteriorate. Being there for her at every moment she was needed. Taking care of Shelly's three kids when her husband Lee needed to be with her. And now this. Debs was sitting sideways on the bed sobbing, really sobbing, a horrid deep cry which made my two daughters start crying in turn. I grabbed her and we all hugged as we sat on the bed. We then fell onto the bed together – me, Deby, Abby and Megan – in a big, tearful hug. Lee, standing at the end of the bed, was the only person not in tears. 'I've got cancer, mate' I repeated to him. He just looked back at me, hurting. We both knew that Shelly was only weeks away from death herself. Then he, too, broke down in uncontrollable sobs.

After Lee and my family left the hospital, I experienced the longest night of my life. The next day I would face a scan which would reveal how far the cancer had spread. All sorts of frantic and silly questions were running through my head. I was facing death, it seemed, and so I started to worry about the contingencies. 'Who's going to lock the doors at night?' 'Who's going to look after my girls?' 'Who's going to look after my parents?' 'Who's going to give my girls away on their wedding days?' 'What's my funeral going to be like?' 'How will Deby cope?' And still the blood clots kept coming, a slow and steady trickle of jam from my penis.

I was soon told that I would have to wait 'five or six weeks' to have the kidney removed. Scan results indicated that the cancer was confined to my kidney, but they couldn't be sure if it had spread or not until they operated. While I was waiting to get shot of the organ, all sorts of emotions were running through my head. Life, mortality, identity, all sorts. Those five or six weeks were, without question, the worst of my life. At times, I was very down, lost in introspection, wondering what it was all about. Lying in my hospital bed, mulling over the fact that I had cancerous tumour on my kidney, then mulling it over again. And again. And again. All my struggles, all my hopes and dreams, my achievements, my disappointments, all seemed to merge in to one pitiful sigh. If it wasn't for the massive support from my family, I'm not sure whether my inner resolve to fight the disease would have prevailed. At times, I was extremely low.

After the diagnosis, the last thing I wanted was sympathy; I wanted to fight, not to wallow in people's condolences. Having said that, I was touched by how many former footballers called me for a chat after hearing my news. Some I would consider close friends and some I wouldn't. Regardless, most of the members of that unique band of brothers formed over my decade of Irish service phoned me up. It's not easy to speak to someone who is miserable and so I am mightily grateful to them for having the guts and the heart to do so. My great friend Alan Kelly offered me wonderful support, as did friends like Andy Awford and Andy Thomson. Then there were those who I hadn't played alongside who nonetheless called to wish me well: players from before my time like Liam Brady (in my opinion one of the greatest players ever to pull on the green jersey of Ireland) who had taken his final bow on the Ireland stage before I'd even earned my first cap.

Then there were a few people I expected to hear from, but who never called. Plenty, in fact. People find it hard to find words fitting for such bad news. There were some former teammates who didn't call and even some fairly close family members. Sometimes people don't realise the immense power of a simple text message to lift you when you are deep down.

I was surprised at the Football Association of Ireland. In 2007, aged forty, I underwent a hip replacement: testament to the fact that for twenty years I had put my body on the line for club and country, particularly the latter. I had always dutifully turned out for the Republic. I was there for those exhausting, eye-reddening foreign trips. I'd put up with the corner-cutting and the occasionally poor hotels that the FAI laid on for its players and I'd never kicked up a fuss. God knows, I'd have slept outside the hotel on a park bench if I'd had to! Even if I didn't get a game, it was an honour to be picked to represent my country. And then, beyond the privilege of playing for Ireland, just think how much money my goal that put us into USA '94 made the FAI! How many corporate junkets were carved out of my left foot volley? In short, I'd done the state some service. My body was testament to that story. Bruises. Sprains. Torn muscles. Prolapsed disc. Dodgy hip. And now, most seriously of all, this. So, did the FAI put in a courtesy call or merely a letter when I was at my lowest ebb? No they didn't!

Amidst the misery of my condition, I was certain of one thing. The care I received via the British public health system was first rate. It made me value the principle of free-at-the-point-of-delivery care that comes with the British National Health Service, and all that it stands for. At one stage in my treatment, the NHS transferred me to a private BUPA hospital in Bristol for a couple of days. Laid up in bed there, a knock came at the door. It was a smartly dressed middle aged woman, all shoulder pads and lipstick, who introduced herself as from BUPA's marketing department. They had heard that a former professional footballer was in the hospital and wanted to publicise the fact by covering it in their magazine. I agreed to do an interview, but there were a few preliminaries, she explained. First of all, she wanted to know, how long had I been a BUPA customer? I told her that I was, in fact, an NHS patient. Very quickly, she cancelled the interview, gathered her things, and left the room. Right, I thought, I'm nothing more than a commodity. And that, for me, encapsulates the difference between public and private health care.

And then there was Shelly. I saw her often in the last weeks of her fight with breast cancer, which were simultaneously my first weeks of the fight. Those meetings were achingly bitter-sweet. I was tremendously grateful of her support and benefited from her experience in fighting the disease. My cancer helped me to understand what she was going through with hers. We held hands and we spoke. Shared the struggle. Shared the pain. Shared the fear. All the time, though, she was getting worse and worse. I tried to shut out this realisation, although it was becoming more evident every single time we met. I loved Shelly, as did Deby, Abby and Megan, and our common fight had drawn me closer to her. I desperately wanted her to pull through; to give hope to Lee, to their kids, to her family. And, of course, to me. It sounds selfish, but watching her get progressively closer to death was like a premonition of what might await me. But I tried my absolute hardest to remain upbeat as we chatted away on those occasions, holding her hand and willing her to miraculously rally back.

• • •

One evening, 10 October 2012, to be exact, I was in Portsmouth at a personal development review (PDR) evening with kids aged 11 to 16. PDRs are carried out every six weeks and are when parents and youth players get news on their progress. They are a bit like a school parents' evening and come complete with a written review. I shouldn't really have been back at work at all. Just four weeks earlier I'd been diagnosed with cancer and I was supposed to be preparing for a forthcoming operation to try and remove it. But I wanted to show the kids, parents and staff at the Portsmouth Academy that I was OK, and so I turned up that evening, and gave the detailed feedback each young player deserved. I called Deby after the PDR meeting. Megan answered the phone. 'Mum can't talk', she said, 'she's driving us to the hospice'. Since it was 9:30pm at night I knew what was unfolding in front us. Shelly was slipping away, it was time to say goodbye. So I raced back from Portsmouth to Swindon.

Deby had effectively been looking after two families for the last year while Shelly was ailing and so, after saying their final goodbyes to Shelly, Deby left the hospice with our girls, Megan and Abby, and Simone, Ava and Bryce (Lee and Shelly's children). I stayed and sat with Shelly and Lee all night in the hospice. The doctors had given her a 'driver': a combination of powerful drugs to make the last few hours a bit more bearable. Realising she was slipping away in front of our eyes was dreadful, but I didn't want to leave her. Lee, however, insisted that I went home. I was having my pre-op assessment in Bristol at 10am the next day. It was therefore imperative that my blood pressure was at a normal level. For it to be so, I should have been avoiding any stressful situations. But this, for me, was exceptional. Lee, though, was insistent. He pointed out that I would fail the assessment and miss out on my operation if I didn't go home and get some sleep. By 5.30am he had finally convinced me to leave and I got in the car and headed home. I crept in the door of my house ten minutes later, not wanting to wake Deby and the girls, if they were asleep at all. By 5:45am I was on the settee and felt my heavy eyelids closing. Sleep. Merciful sleep. Five minutes later, at 5:50am, I was awoken by Deby. Lee had just called. Shelly was dead.

I pulled my clothes back on immediately and made it to the hospice for 6am. I wanted to stay with Lee all day to support him through his grief but I had to leave him just two hours later, rushing home for a quick shower before driving up the motorway to Bristol for my pre-op. That was a very emotional drive to make but Deby, as ever, was by my side. My blood pressure was, unsurprisingly, very high but once Deby told the medical team the circumstances, they understood and gave the go-ahead for me to have my kidney removed four days later.

The operation took place on 16 October 2012. As a professional footballer, I was well used to operations. I'd had eight or so before which had involved being put to sleep. So I was fairly calm about the operation itself. In fact, going into the operating theatre, I wasn't scared at all. I just felt an overwhelming sense of relief that this horrible growth inside me would finally be removed. Before the operation the doctors told me that, going by the scan, they didn't think it had spread. Then again, they couldn't be sure. Even before this positive step, that same old niggling doubt. I just braced myself for the surgery and, as the drowsiness came, fell into a welcome unconsciousness.

While I was asleep, the surgeon – Dr Frank Keeley – performed a keyhole operation involving two small incisions in my stomach. Keyhole operations are Dr Keeley's speciality. He first bagged my kidney and then removed it. It came out through my groin, leaving a four inch scar.

After waking up, I anxiously waited for news from the surgeon. I had only been six weeks since I'd first passed blood. Still, those six weeks seemed more like six months. Dr Keeley told me that he thought it had been a successful procedure. But, as they always say, 'we'll have to wait and see'. He then asked me if I would like to participate in a drugs trial for a new drug by the wonderfully unpronounceable name of Sorafenib, which was being developed to treat primary cancers of the kidney and liver. There was some evidence, he told me, that Sorafenib reduces tumours in kidneys and they needed people of the right age and with the right physical anomalies to test it. 'Would you be interested in helping other people in your condition, Mr McLoughlin?' he asked. I instantly agreed. I was so genuinely grateful to the power of medical science that if he'd have asked me to participate in a trial which involved eating horse manure for the next five years, I'd have said 'yes'.

Shelly had passed away four days before I had the kidney removed. But Lee waited to bury her because he wanted me to carry the coffin. That meant that Shelly wasn't buried until 29 October 2012, which was the first available date. I was honoured that Lee had asked me to carry Shelly into the crematorium and took to my task at the front of the pall bearers. I was still suffering pain and anxiety following the operation, but I had to put my feelings behind me and be there for Lee and his family. As I was to be right at the front, I wanted to do it properly. While walking up the aisle, I was conscious that there would be people in the funeral congregation talking about me, looking at me to see how I was doing physically. So I resisted my physical need to limp and walked tall and stiffly. I was grateful to Lee for waiting until I was fit again to bury Shelly. But for my poor youngest girl, Megan, it meant that her 18th birthday happened to coincide with the funeral. On the day on which we should have been celebrating Megan's transition into adulthood, we were in fact grieving her 'Auntie' Shelly. It meant that Megan's big day – her one and only 18th – would forever hold painful memories.

Four weeks after Shelly was cremated, I started the drug trial: a little act of altruism which I undertook not merely in recognition of my struggle with cancer, but also Shelly's and millions of other people's. When I first was administered Sorafenib, I didn't know if I'd been given the placebo or the drug itself. After two weeks, however, I knew it was the real deal. I had been warned that the side effects could be aggressive, but I was still a bit shocked at the physical effects it had on me. First, the skin on my feet and hands became dry. Then, my blood pressure started slowly creeping up. I also needed to go to the toilet more frequently and more urgently. At this stage I was on two tablets a day. But the trial, which is a three year course of tablets, involved upping the dosage to four tablets a day. After switching to four tablets a day, my feet really began to ache. Then, within ten days, my hair fell out. I acquired a big bald patch and what was left of my hair was seriously thin. It was as if, having escaped the need for radiotherapy or chemotherapy, I was now suffering the effects of it. Also, now when I needed to go to the toilet I really needed to go. I've a long motorway commute to work from Swindon to Portsmouth and so, on more than one occasion, I had to floor it to get to the next service station, quickly park up the car, and run awkwardly towards the toilets, barging past people to make it to the pan on time.

With my hair falling out in clumps thanks to good old Sorafenib, I decided to shave my head. I went down to TK Maxx and bought a full shaving kit. But when home, while looking in the mirror and trying to shave hair at the same time, I shaved into my eyebrow. I got quite upset at that point. I constantly had the runs, my hair had fallen out, and my blood pressure was dangerously high. And on top of it all, I couldn't even shave my head without removing an eyebrow in the process. I felt wretched. And then, I started to pity myself again. And that's when I knew that I had to go back to the hospital and speak to the doctors. I was determined to carry on with the trial, but told the doctors what I was going through. How it was affecting my recovery, mentally as much as physically. They asked me if I wanted to stop taking Sorafenib. I answered 'no'. Morally, for me, it would have been the wrong thing to do. So we agreed to reduce my dosage to two tablets a day. I remain on the drug and will be until January 2016. I have to take immodium every three or four days to cope with my dodgy tummy and I will have to take tablets for the rest of my life due to its effects on my blood pressure. But as long as I can do my small bit to save the lives of people going through what I did, it's certainly worth it.

They removed my kidney and with it, hopefully, the cancer. Hope is the operative word there. The operation was a success, yes. The prognosis is good, true. But when they take the organ away, they say they think they've got it all out. Even now, there is a question mark. I just have to live with that. But I feel optimistic. The scans are clear and the signs are good. You seize on the positives and move forward. That's what you've got to do. If my life experience has taught me one thing it's that you have got to take things head on. Knuckle down and deal with the discomfort. The one thing I didn't want, that I don't want, is sympathy. I said that right from the off and the main reason is this: I don't want people to feel uncomfortable around me. At the risk of sounding clichéd, life can be hard. Very hard. Faced with this reality, family and friends are invaluable. Deby, in particular, has been around to give me a kick in the arse when I'm feeling too sorry for myself and a cuddle when appropriate. She's been at my side whenever I've felt that sense of impending doom before getting results. There for me during every hospital visit. During every low point. During every agonising wait, when the computer screen slowly comes up with your results. On a personal level, too, a positive mental attitude is imperative. You just have to take the blows on the chin and carry on the battle. To achieve that, unfortunately, you sometimes have to simply trick your mind into thinking upbeat. That, and keep busy. But the latter, of course, was never a problem for me.

Revolution on the south coast

With that attitude driving me on, I returned to work prematurely. Although today I'm immensely proud to be first team coach at a club with the history and passion of Portsmouth, the day-to-day reality is hardly glamorous. I drive a mud-flecked white van to training. Inside is all the training equipment: bibs, plastic cones, metal dummies, and the like. When I arrive at the university pitches where we're based, I fling the doors open and the players crowd around to help me shift the stuff out. It's not quite 'magic sponge' and sucking oranges at half time, but it's not far off.

The lack of infrastructure at the club can be traced back to the champagne-soaked complacency when Pompey were enjoying the highs of Premiership football and FA Cup success. But in 2011, with their club about to be made extinct, the fans organised and fought back. The Pompey Supporters' Trust stepped in and, with the help of the City Council, wrested back control of their football team and their stadium. Portsmouth FC is now the largest fan-owned football club in Britain.

Under fan ownership, money is being spent on improving infrastructure rather than inflated salaries: a quarter of a million on the pitch; three quarters of a million on a sprinkler system for the old South Stand. Small investments but meaningful, sustainable investments. Change comes dropping slow, but it's underway. Pompey recently used Tifosy crowd funding to raise £2m, which was badly needed for the club's Academy. The difference with the current Portsmouth model is that the club is being run by people who love and care for the club, from the board of directors right down to Big Kev the kit man. I've taken several pay cuts in my various roles at the club and I returned to work long before it was medically advisable to do so. I've stayed on and served Pompey. For richer, for poorer. In sickness and in health. Why? Because Portsmouth fans are second to none. The city is an enclave where love for the club runs deep in the blood. In very few British cities the size of Portsmouth will you drive round the streets and notice that every kid you come across is in his home town strip: no Man United or Man City jerseys, just the blue of Pompey.

I could have played it safe and turned down a coaching role. I was very aware when I took up a senior position at the club that I would one day face the sack. My career has taught me that coaches and managers live a precarious existence and that longevity in the job is very rare indeed. Similarly, I could have thrown in the towel when cancer came knocking. But there is a spirit about this football club that is seductive; it's a bitter-sweet and passionate love which, once you embrace it fully, becomes very difficult to divorce yourself from.

After I went public with my cancer diagnosis, I received many messages of support from Pompey fans. One stuck out. It was from a man named Steve Howden, a big Portsmouth fan who was waiting to have the very same operation as me. He had read my story in the Portsmouth Evening News and emailed to wish me luck. That was the start of an email correspondence where we offered each other mutual support. Steve's operation was scheduled for two weeks after mine so, after Dr Keeley had worked his magic with me, I was able to tell Steve what to expect. Unfortunately, Steve's cancer had spread and just months after undergoing surgery he passed away. I joined his family at the unveiling of a plaque to him on Pompey's memorial wall at Fratton Park. Portsmouth Football Club has enabled such personal bonds to take place. Bonds which otherwise would not have existed and which have helped me through.

Yet when I do eventually get the sack, which I inevitably will, I will look on my legacy at Pompey with pride. I went back to a club that I love in order to influence, mould and build; to take it to new levels; and to give younger players the benefit of my long experience in the game. Together with manager Andy Awford, whom I played alongside at the club and has been a great friend to me through thick and thin for over twenty-two years, we have brought fans back and we've restored a sense of what Pompey is all about: a hub, a focal point, a place to be proud off. In short, I want to be part of the revolution. And, to be sure, what's happening at Pompey is nothing short of a revolution in the way football clubs are owned and run. It is a model that will be replicated all over England and Europe. I'm certain of that. A plaque erected by fans outside the ground sums it up:

'We cannot change the past but we can shape the future'.

That shows the power of hope and resolve, which function even in the teeth of desperation. Even the most hard-bitten cynic would struggle to find fault with the positivity and togetherness that characterise the club at this revolutionary time.

Naturally, Portsmouth Football Club is not full of exclusively good memories for me. Occasionally I have to go to the toilet in the away changing room at Fratton Park. Returning to the place where I first passed blood is an eerie experience and I try to avoid it. But it also reminds me of how different my story could have been had I ignored the blood and grimaced through the pain. Had I, say, just self-anaesthetised myself with alcohol and waited for the blood clots to pass. Had I blocked it out mentally, as most of us would usually do, and carried on with my busy life. If I'd done that, I'm sure I wouldn't be here today. So if you are reading this, and you've passed blood in your urine, please – please – do get it checked out. Thinking positively and keeping busy is fine, but if it means completely avoiding reality in the process, it can be very dangerous.

My role at Portsmouth today is hands-on and I rarely have a spare moment. But when I do find myself at home, flicking between television channels, or just feeling a little bit down, I occasionally get out the video of that goal against Northern Ireland. I watch my volley and I watch the elation on my face as I wheel away from hitting the goal. Then I think back to touching down at Dublin airport as the hero of the hour. And then I think back over my life and over my career. Serious illness brings with it the inevitable thought of standing at the pearly gates and accounting for your life. So I think back on the characters I've come across; the family members I've loved and cherished; the joy and the pain. I think back to Big Jack telling the cameras that, with that goal, I'd justified my existence. And I reflect, with a wry smile, that yes, when all is said and done, I've done exactly that.

ALAN McLOUGHLIN'S CLUB RECORD

CLUB	FROM	TO	FEE	LEAGUE Apps/Goals	FA CUP Apps/Goals	LGE CUP Apps/Goals	OTHER Apps/Goals
Man Utd	25 Apr, 85	15 Aug, 86	Apprentice	0 (0)/0	0 (0)/0	0 (0)/0	0 (0)/0
Swindon	15 Aug, 86	13 Dec, 90	Free	101 (5)/19	4 (2)/0	11 (3)/5	10 (0)/1
Torquay	13 Mar, 87	13 Aug, 87	Loan	16 (0)/1	0 (0)/0	0 (0)/0	0 (0)/0
Torquay	14 Aug, 87	30 Sep, 88	Loan	5 (3)/3	0 (0)/0	0 (0)/0	0 (0)/0
Southampton	13 Dec, 90	17 Feb, 92	£1,000,000	22 (2)/1	4 (0)/0	0 (1)/0	1 (0)/0
Aston Villa	30 Sep, 91	3 Oct, 91	Loan	0 (0)/0	0 (0)/0	0 (0)/0	1 (0)/0
Portsmouth	17 Feb, 92	09 Dec, 99	£400,000	297 (12)/54	15 (1)/7	27 (0)/7	9 (0)/1
Wigan	09 Dec, 99	25 Oct, 01	£260,000	13 (10)/1	0 (0)/ 0	0 (1)/0	5 (0)/2
Rochdale	20 Dec, 01	29 May, 02	Free	17 (3)/1	0 (0)/0	0 (0)/0	0 (0)/0
Forest Green	12 Jul, 02	01 Jun, 03	Free	10 (2)/0	0 (0) 0	0 (0)/0	0 (0)/0
TOTALS			**£1,660,000**	**481 (37)/80**	**23 (3)/7**	**38 (5)/12**	**26 (0)/4**
Goals per Game				0.15	0.26	n/a	0.15

INTERNATIONAL RECORD

Republic of Ireland, 1990–1999, 42 caps, 2 goals

Player of the Year, 1996

THE BEST IRELAND TEAM ALAN McLOUGHLIN PLAYED ALONGSIDE

Shay Given

Denis Irwin **Paul McGrath** **Kevin Moran** **Steve Staunton**

Roy Keane **Ronnie Whelan**

Ray Houghton **Andy Townsend**

Robbie Keane **John Aldridge**

INDEX

ABOUT BRYCE EVANS

Dr Bryce Evans is Senior Lecturer in History at Liverpool Hope University and Winston Churchill Fellow. A graduate of the University of Warwick and University College Dublin, he is also a lifelong Portsmouth and Republic of Ireland supporter and Alan McLoughlin is his hero.

His published works include the books Seán Lemass: Democratic Dictator (2012), Frank Aiken: Nationalist and Internationalist, and Ireland during the Second World War: Farewell to Plato's Cave (both 2014).